What gunpowder did for war, the printing press has done for the mind.

Wendell Phillips (1811-84)

Print Matters
20th Anniversary Edition

THE CUTTING EDGE OF PRINT

First published and distributed by
viction workshop ltd

viction:ary™

viction workshop ltd
Unit C, 7/F, Seabright Plaza, 9-23 Shell Street,
North Point, Hong Kong
Url: www.victionary.com
Email: we@victionary.com
@victionworkshop
@victionworkshop
Bē @victionary
@victionary

Edited and produced by viction:ary

Concept & art direction by Victor Cheung
Book design by viction workshop ltd
Contributing editor: Katee Hui

ISBN 978-988-74629-7-2
Printed and bound in China

PRINT MATTERS

THE CUTTING EDGE OF PRINT

20th Anniviction:ary

Beauty is manifested in the refinement of functionality—and then everything reappears anew.

Felix Ng
Anonymous

FOREWORD

I first came across print effects on an instant noodle packaging from a convenience store in Tokyo, Japan. In order to remove hot water from the box when the noodles are ready, perforations were made on one side of its cover, which allowed me to drain the water with little effort. That moment changed my entire perspective of what design is and should be. A simple print effect of perforated holes on a box of instant noodle delivers an important lesson on design. It performs a considerate act to, or rather a reconsideration of, the product and its consumers. Beauty is manifested in the refinement of functionality—and then everything reappears anew.

Design is a logical process, and yet designers constantly challenge themselves with the task of defying logic through the delivery of unexpected ideas that surprise people in a way that enhances how we have been living before.

Now, more than ever, an increasingly wide range of materials, finishing and print techniques are made available to us. There are more choices and options at our disposal that grant design a flexibility that it never had before; we can now do somersaults in places where we used to stumble. A print effect ultimately remains a technique. It is the usage of an effect or technique that transpires concepts.
A good print effect is one that is appropriated in a way that accentuates the functionality of a product and its concepts. After all, agility is nothing without creative dexterity. The biggest challenge ahead of us isn't what we haven't done but how we can use it to transform the mundane to the extraordinary. So take what you can get and run.

Use this book. Abuse it. Read every single word on the projects featured in this book from the front to its back. Add sticky notes. Do whatever you want with it. Just don't relegate it to a pretty (boring) life on the bookshelf. Look beyond the beauty of the works and dig deeper to see why certain print techniques, effects or materials were used to communicate or enhance a concept — or even function as the concept itself, much like the perforations of an instant noodle packaging.

FOREWORD

It's all about creating unique results after all, and this would not be possible solely with a digital printer. I used to use a traditional offset machine, feeding paper sheets straight into the rollers to produce visual signs directly on the printer.

My first attempt to use the "water random offset printing", which I refer to as the WROP effect, was for the Blackswan Foundation's visual identity in 2010. Blackswan is dedicated to researching rare diseases, and WROP was a technique specially developed to generate unpredictable patterns that can be as unique as the rare cases of the orphan diseases. For their leaflet cover, I used a dark red to evoke a kind of revolutionary feel.

WROP made a second appearance in 2013 on the posters and leaflets for Lausanne Underground Film & Music Festival (LUFF) featured in this book. We played with the institutional identity of the festival, using black lines in the middle of the letter as the negation of the logo itself. This idea of "underground is no longer underground", the aesthetics of censorship and concealed signs were all the starting point of the LUFF campaign. We reversed the method so that black bands would render a "subversive" festival instead. "Accident" was also the theme of LUFF 13, so the technique was the perfect answer for the project.

Our next target is to explore colour interaction and saturation with only CMY inks going into the machine. The project will be soon released under a form of a video.

Exploration and experimentation are key to these kind of projects. "Hacking", "do it yourself", "random" and "craftsmanship" are all key parts of the research process that have been hidden over the last two decades, an era in which everything became digitalised and over–standardised and the values of experimentation were absent. The great chef Massimo Bottura asserted that innovation sometimes involves taking two steps backwards to go forward. I think that resonate in the WROP projects.

Innovation sometimes involves taking two steps backwards to go forward. I think that resonates in the WROP projects.

Demian Conrad

Index of Printing & production techniques

CONTENTS

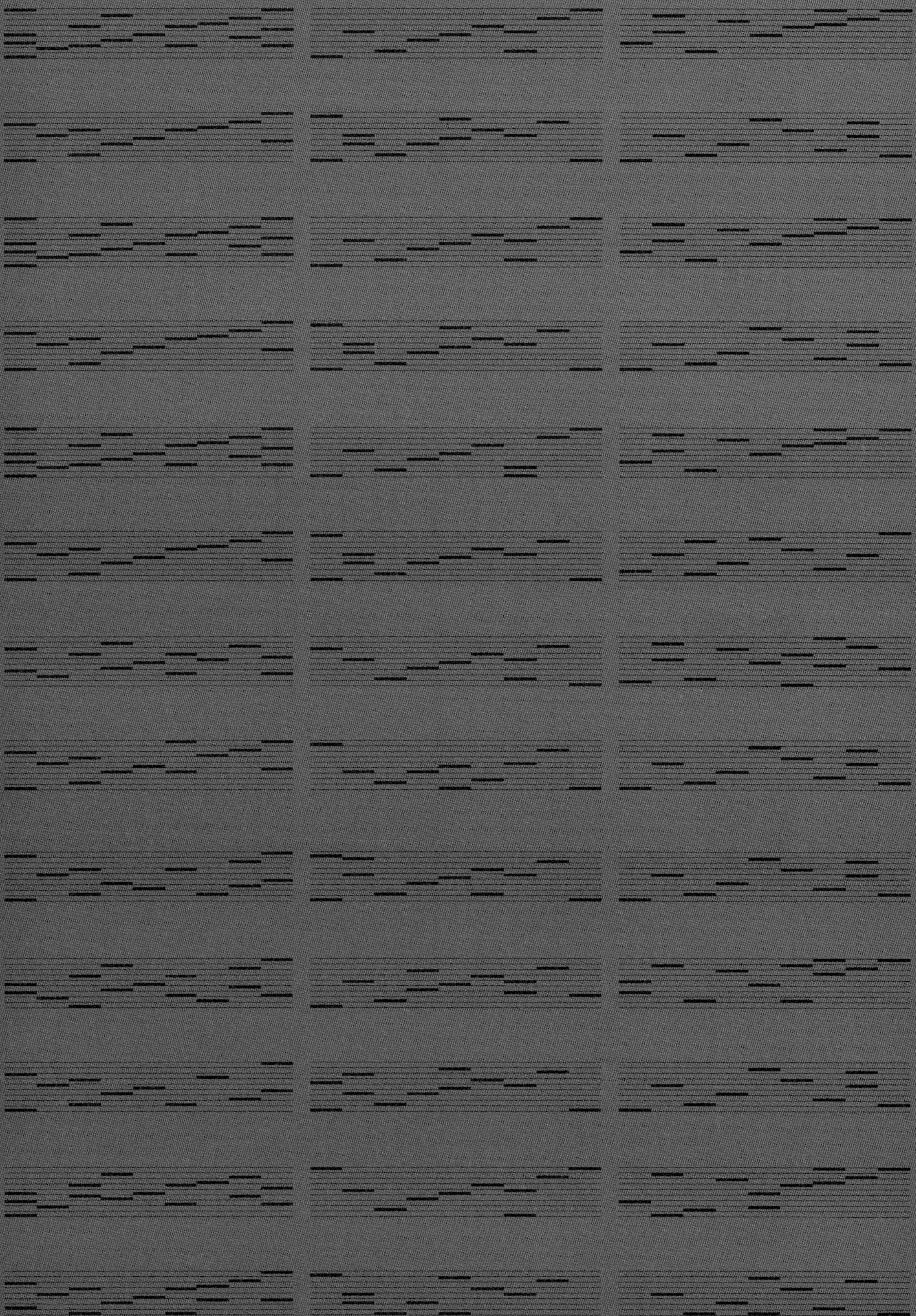

Branding & Identities

Branding & Identities

Branding & Identities

Branding & Identities

Branding & Identities

Branding & Identities

Branding & Identities

Branding & Identities

Branding & Identities

House of Wang brand identity

— .Oddity Studio

House of Wang is an interior gallery with a focus on state-of-the-art furniture, bringing brands like Se, Orche and Apparatus to the Beijing market. For its visual identity, the team at .Oddity Studio created a sharp avant-garde inspired logo mark using the brand name's initials to stress its core essence. Simple lines form the symbol and work as the main graphical element used to brand any communication material, resembling alien typography that goes well with selected furniture artworks.

Client House of Wang
Effects Hot Stamping, embossing & debossing

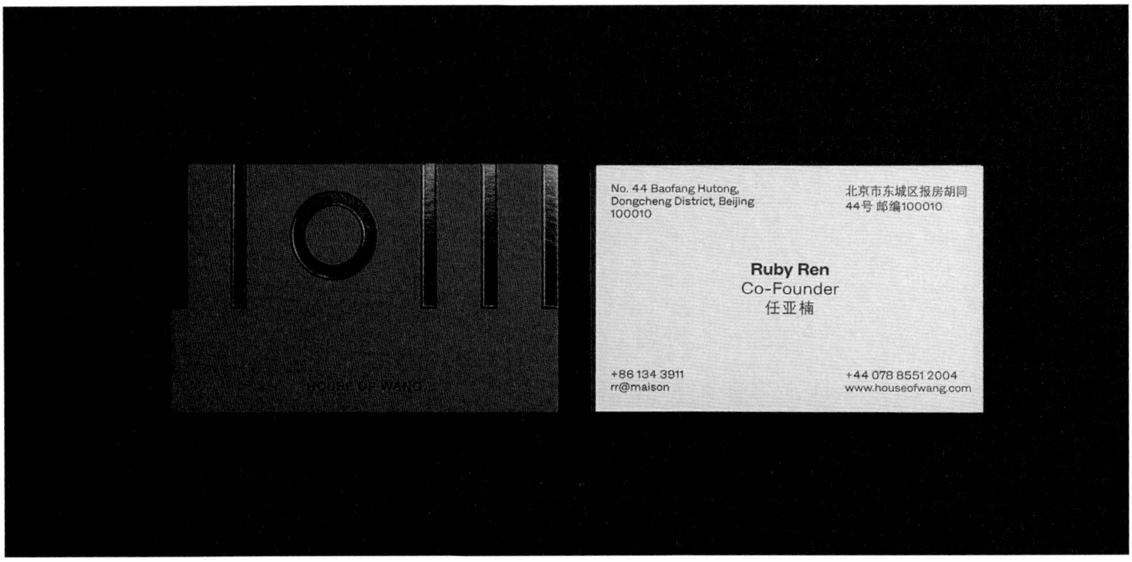

No. 44 Baofang Hutong,
Dongcheng District, Beijing 100010
HOUSE OF WANG
北京市东城区报房胡同
44号 邮编100010
No. 44 Baofang Hutong,
Dongcheng District, Beijing 100010
HOUSE OF WANG
北京市东城区报房胡同
44号 邮编100010

HOUSE OF WANG

Lavaderos

— Anagrama

Named after Los Lavaderos de Almoloya, a traditional wash house that ran under its current venue, Lavaderos is a bar in Puebla Mexico that immerses customers in a unique experience where history meets sophistication. Tasked with designing its visual identity, Anagrama were inspired by the colonial culture of the city to integrate classic label aesthetics and old occult art engravings into a more modern paradigm. The logo varieties and illustrations exude an alchemical feel to create a sense of mystery and intrigue.

Client Lavaderos
Effects Hot stamping, embossing & debossing, non-paper materials

Lavaderos

Lavaderos

Rosewood Puebla
8 ORIENTE No. 1012
PASEO DE SAN FRANCISCO
COLONIA BARRIO EL ALTO
Puebla, Puebla, CP 72000
+52 (81) 222 122 2300 www.rosewoodhotels.com

LAVADEROS

Due Brothers

— Mubien

Due Brothers is a family-owned full-service construction company that specialises in solar and panel installations in San Diego. For its visual identity, Mubien drew on a vintage look-and-feel to create a new aesthetic for the industry, with the design of its business cards simulating the characteristic pattern of solar panels. The materials and colour palette played an important role in the project, while the stationery is handmade using different glossy black hot-foil patterns and dry bas-reliefs.

Client Due Brothers
Collaboration Workshop Built
Effects Hot Stamping, embossing & debossing

ESTD DUE 2008
BROTHERS
DO SOLAR
Adam Due
Co-Founder
Mobile
480.399.4311
E-mail
adam@duebrothers.com

ESTD DUE 2008
BROTHERS
DO SOLAR
Co-Founder
480.399.4311
adam@duebrothers.com

DO SOLAR
Co-Founder
480.399.4311
adam@duebrothers.com

DUE
BROTHERS

Co-Founder
Adam Due - Co-Founder
Adam Due - Co-Founder

ESTD DUE 2008
BROTHERS
DO SOLAR
San Diego, CA 92107
www.duebrothers.com
Adam Due - Co-Founder

ESTO DUE 2008
BROTHERS
GO SOLAR
Adam Due
Co-Founder
Mobile
480.399.4311
E-mail
adam@duebrothers.com

ESTO DUE 2008
BROTHERS
GO SOLAR

ESTO DUE 2008
BROTHERS
GO SOLAR

Jennifer

— Mubien

Jennifer is a San Diego-based luxury residential real estate agent specialising in some of the most sought-after places to live in the US. In designing a brand identity for her business, the team at Mubien set out to communicate her unique specialties in a sophisticated way while delivering a visual impact aligned with the properties and clientele she represents. The materials and techniques used in producing the stationery (e.g. gold foil stamping, debossing) perfectly represents her dynamic character, commitment to excellence and personalised service.

Client Jennifer
Collaboration Workshop Built
Effects Hot stamping, debossing, edge dipping

RETURN TO
JENNIFER J. JANZEN-BOTTS
16915 AVENIDA DE ACACIAS
RANCHO SANTA FE
CA 92067 / PO BOX 1023
JENNIFER J JANZEN BOTTS
Real expertise for
unreal properties

JENNIFER
eal expertise for
unreal properties
JENNIFER J JANZEN BOTTS

L’envol Fine Dining Restaurant

— .Oddity Studio

L’envol is a French modern fine dining restaurant at St. Regis in Hong Kong. Inspired by the meaning of its name, which can be translated as ‘a take off moment’, the team at .Oddity Sutdio created a visual identity based on the key concept of ‘fine rawness’, which speaks volumes of the chef’s philosophy. The choice of materials and overlays produced unexpected textures and compositions that looked experimental and contemporary yet befitting an elegant eatery reminiscent of traditions.

Client L’envol
Effects Die cutting & perforation, hot stamping, screenprinting

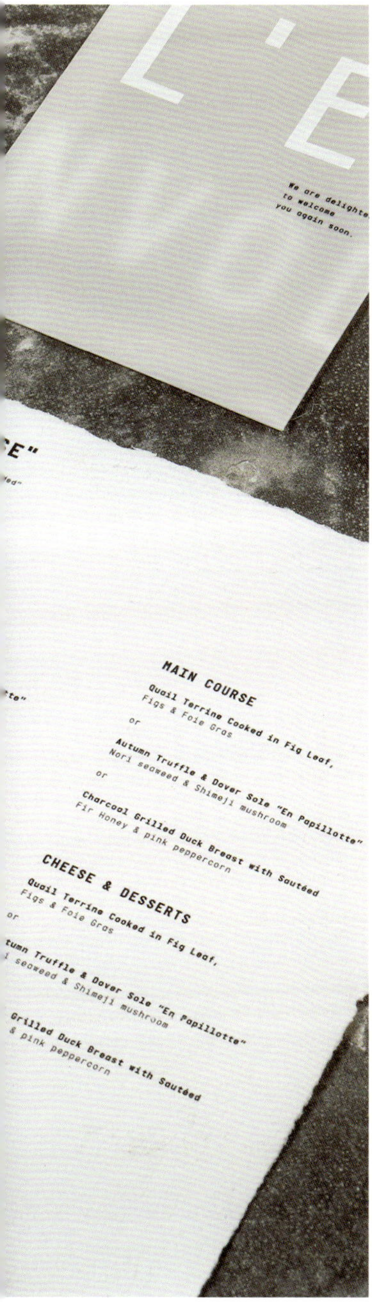
We are delighted
to welcome
you again soon.
MAIN COURSE
Quail Terrine Cooked in Fig Leaf,
Figs & Foie Gras
or
Autumn Truffle & Dover Sole "En Papillotte"
Nori seaweed & Shimeji mushroom
or
Charcoal Grilled Duck Breast with Sautéed
Fir Honey & pink peppercorn
CHEESE & DESSERTS
Quail Terrine Cooked in Fig Leaf,
Figs & Foie Gras
or
Autumn Truffle & Dover Sole "En Papillotte"
Nori seaweed & Shimeji mushroom
Grilled Duck Breast with Sautéed
& pink peppercorn

OLIVIER
ELZER
Culinary Director
+852 1138 681
olivier.elzer@stregis
The St. Regis Hong Kong
3/F, 1 Harbour Drive
Wan Chai
Hong Kong, China
stregishongkong.com
L'ENVOL

NVOL

L'ENVOL
We are delighted
to welcome
you again soon.
"SUR-MESURE"

THANK YOU
Dear Andy,
Many thanks for
being there for our
first "Midnight supper"!
Regards,
J. Pierre

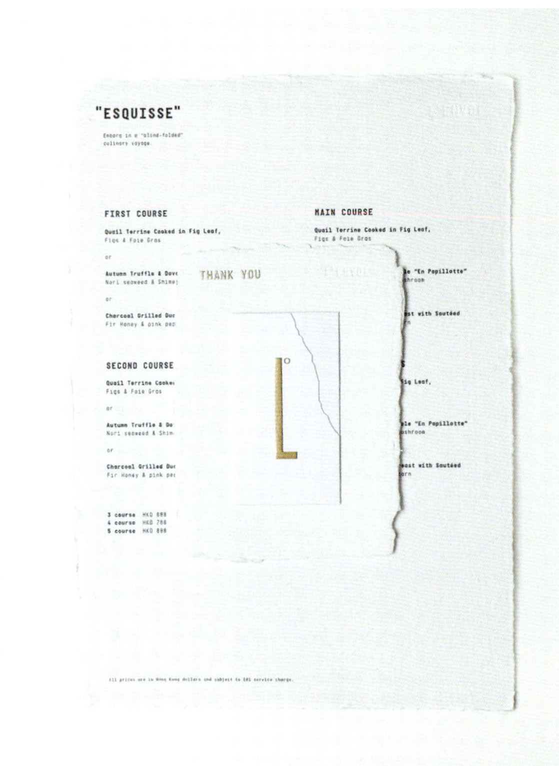
"ESQUISSE"
Embark on a "blind-folded"
culinary voyage.
FIRST COURSE
Quail Terrine Cooked in Fig Leaf,
Figs & Foie Gras
MAIN COURSE
Quail Terrine Cooked in Fig Leaf,
Figs & Foie Gras
SECOND COURSE
THANK YOU
3 course HKD 688
4 course HKD 788
5 course HKD 888

L'ENVOL
INTIMACY OVER
AUSTERITY
COMFORT OVER
CONFORMITY

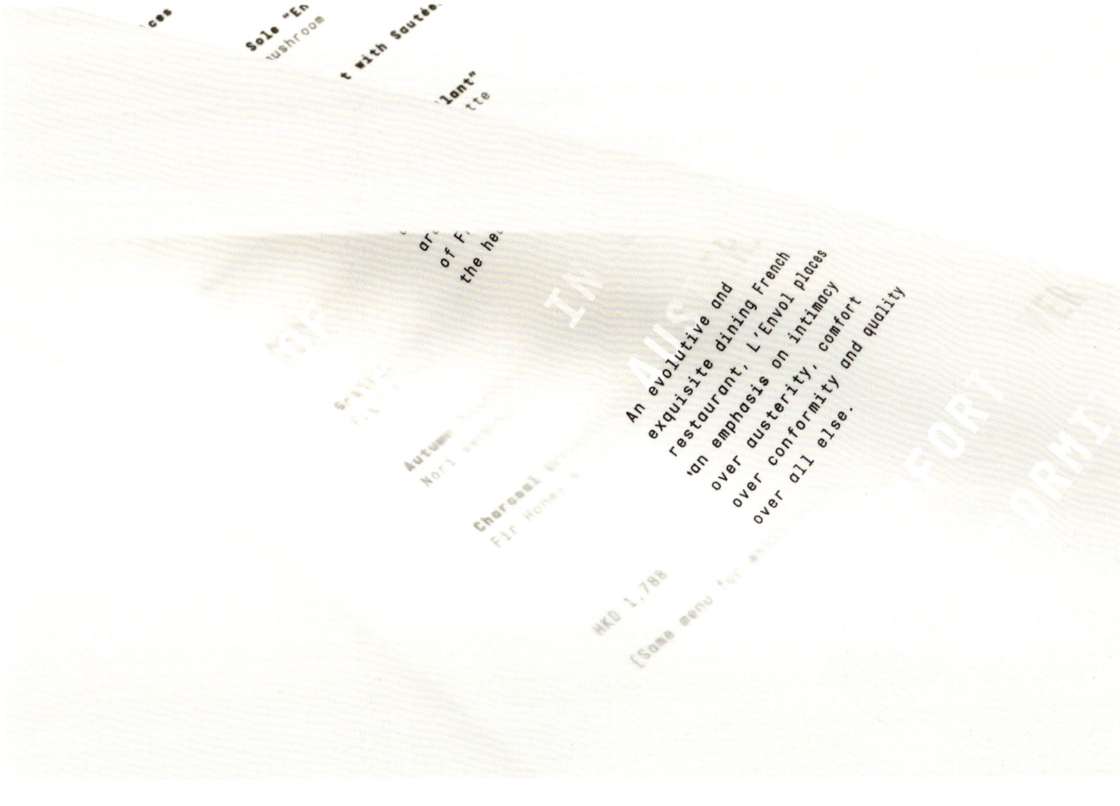
An evolutive and
exquisite dining French
restaurant, L'Envol places
an emphasis on intimacy
over austerity, comfort
over conformity and quality
over all else.

N. Daniels

—Bureau Rabensteiner

Bureau Rabensteiner has designed an "impressive" identity for photo producer Natalie Daniels. Emulating a set of Polaroids in various sizes, the bespoke stationery is varnished with black thermo-sensitive grids that turn white by touch. This simple device relates dynamically to both Daniels' profession and the recipient when they personalise it with imprint.

Client Natalie Daniels
Effects Special ink, screenprinting

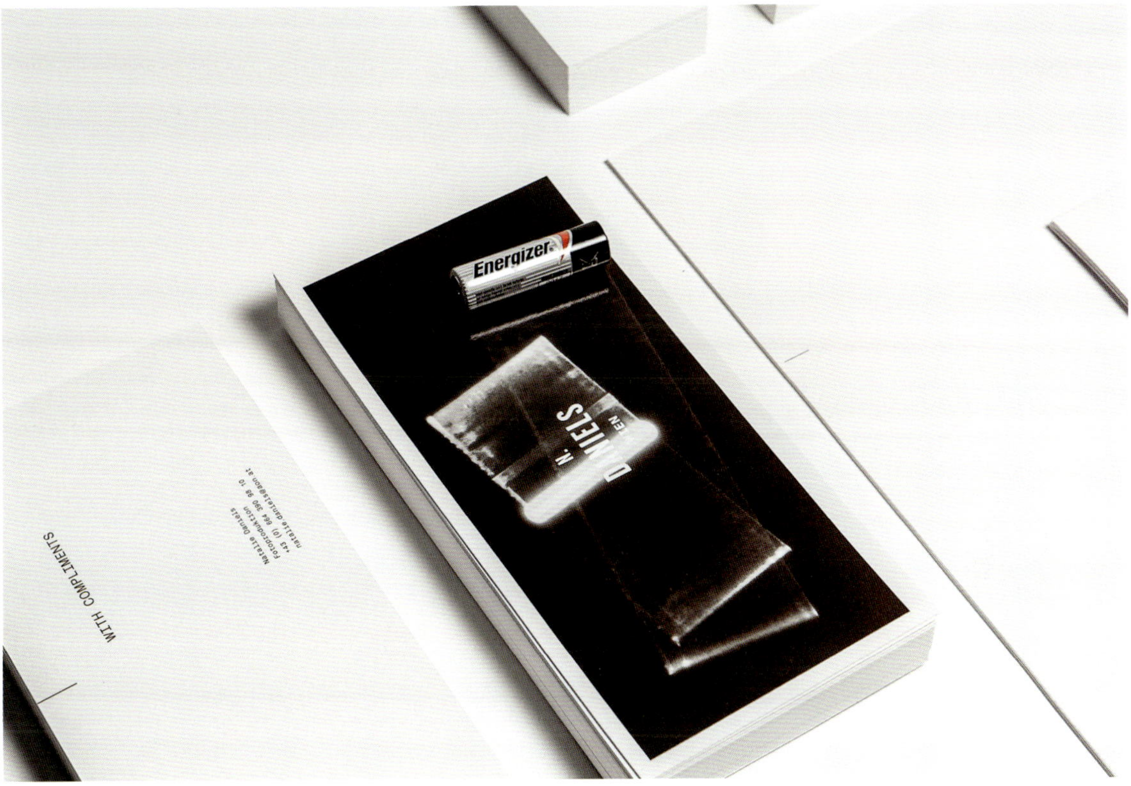
Energizer
N.
DANIELS
WITH COMPLIMENTS

N.
DANIELS
WIEN

N.
DANIELS
WITH COMPLIMENTS

N.
DANIELS
WIEN

N.
DANIELS
WIEN

N.
DANIELS

LUFF 2013

—Demian Conrad Design

Celebrating originality and weirdness, LUFF has been introducing off-the-wall films and relatively unknown music in to mainstream Switzerland. In tune with its 12th edition theme "accident" among others, the festival's communications are tampered with a randomly revealed visual effect. Unsettled between an accidental error or censorship, Water Random Offset Printing (WROP), where visual signs were produced directly on the printing machine, adds noise to the collateral directly during print.

Client Lausanne Underground Film & Music Festival
Effects Technical printing

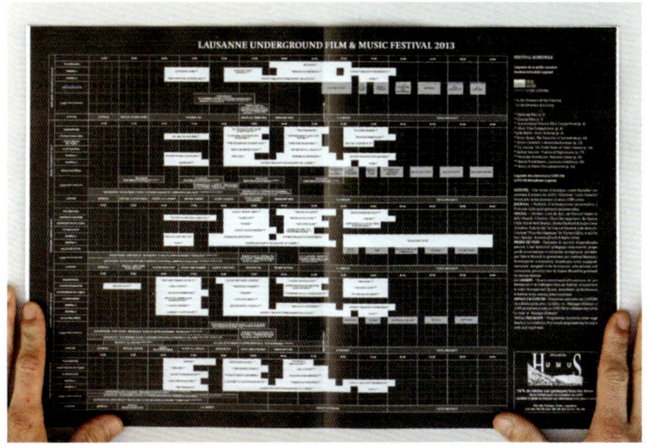
LAUSANNE UNDERGROUND FILM & MUSIC FESTIVAL 2013

LAUSANNE
UNDER
GROUND
FILM&
MUSIC
FESTIVAL
12TH EDITION 16-20.10.13

USANNE
JNDER
ROUND
FILM&
MUSIC
STIVAL
MUSIC
Nicolas Bernier &
Martin Messier
"La Chambre
des machines",
The Haxan Cloak,
Emptyset,
Jello Biafra &
Le Dernier Cri,
Smegma,
FEN (Otomo
Yoshihide,
Yan Jun,
Chee Wai,
Ryu Hankil),
Jean-François
Laporte,
Kiko C. Esseiva,
Leif Elggren,
JG Thirlwell,
ENDON,
Blackphone666,
Jason Lescalleet,
Sajjanu,
VOMIR,
Evil Moisture,
Sugarcraft,
Nate Young
(Wolf Eyes),
and more...
2TH EDITION 16-20.10.13
LUFF.CH

LAUSANNE
UNDER
GROUND
FILM&
MUSIC
FESTIVAL
FILM
Opening Film:
"Bad Film" by
Sion Sono,
Jello Biafra:
Carte Blanche,
The Punk Wave of
Total Cinema,
Walerian
Borowczyk:
Restored Gems,
Marcel Broodthaers:
Cross-Threads,
Eurociné Night,
and more...
WORKSHOPS
L'OFF
LUFF.FM,
exhibitions,
performances,
and more...
MUSIC
Nicolas Bernier &
Martin Messier
"La Chambre
des machines",
The Haxan Cloak,
Yan Jun,
Chee Wai,
Ryu Hankil),
Jean-François
Laporte,
Kiko C. Esseiva,
Leif Elggren,
JG Thirlwell,
ENDON,
Blackphone666,
Jason Lescalleet,
Sajjanu,
VOMIR,
Evil Moisture,
Sugarcraft,
Nate Young
(Wolf Eyes),
and more...
12TH EDITION 16-20.10.13
LUFF.CH

LAUSANNE
UNDER

LAUSANNE
UNDER

UNDER
FILM&
MUSIC
ESTIVAL
The Haxan Cloak,
Emptyset,
Jello Biafra &
Le Dernier Cri,
Smegma,
JG Thirlwell,
ENDON,
Blackphone666,
Jason Lescalleet,
Sajjanu,
VOMIR,
Evil Moisture,
Sugarcraft,
Nate Young
(Wolf Eyes),
and more...
12TH EDITION 16–20.10.13
LUFF.CH

MUSIC

A Design Film Festival 2014

—Anonymous

Conceived by Anonymous, the fourth edition of A Design Film Festival was themed "On a Scale of Art to Design". Looking at scale as less of a measure but more the vast spectrum of creative works, the festival's identity contrasts the breadth of works through a black and white palette. On it an amalgam of geometric shapes and lines is animated by varnish, denoting all of design's main discourses and subcultures, stances and nuances shown in the year's featured movies.

Client A Design Film Festival
Effects Die cutting & perforation, spot colour, UV varnishing

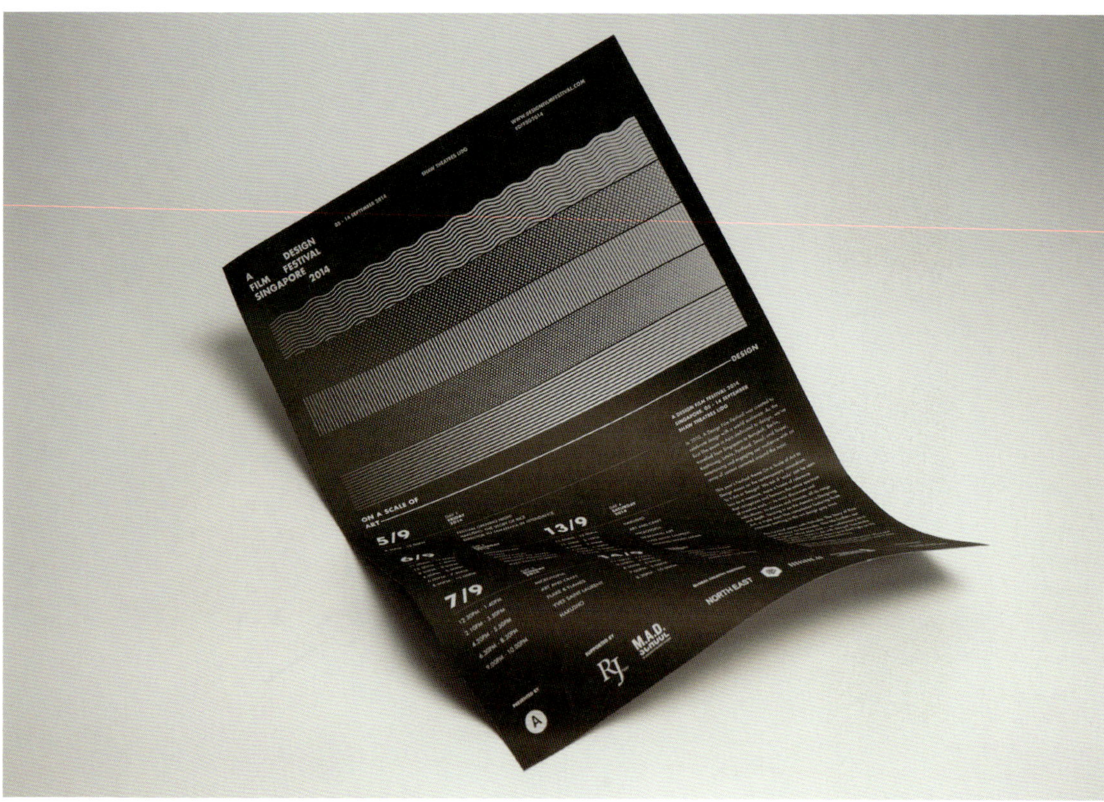

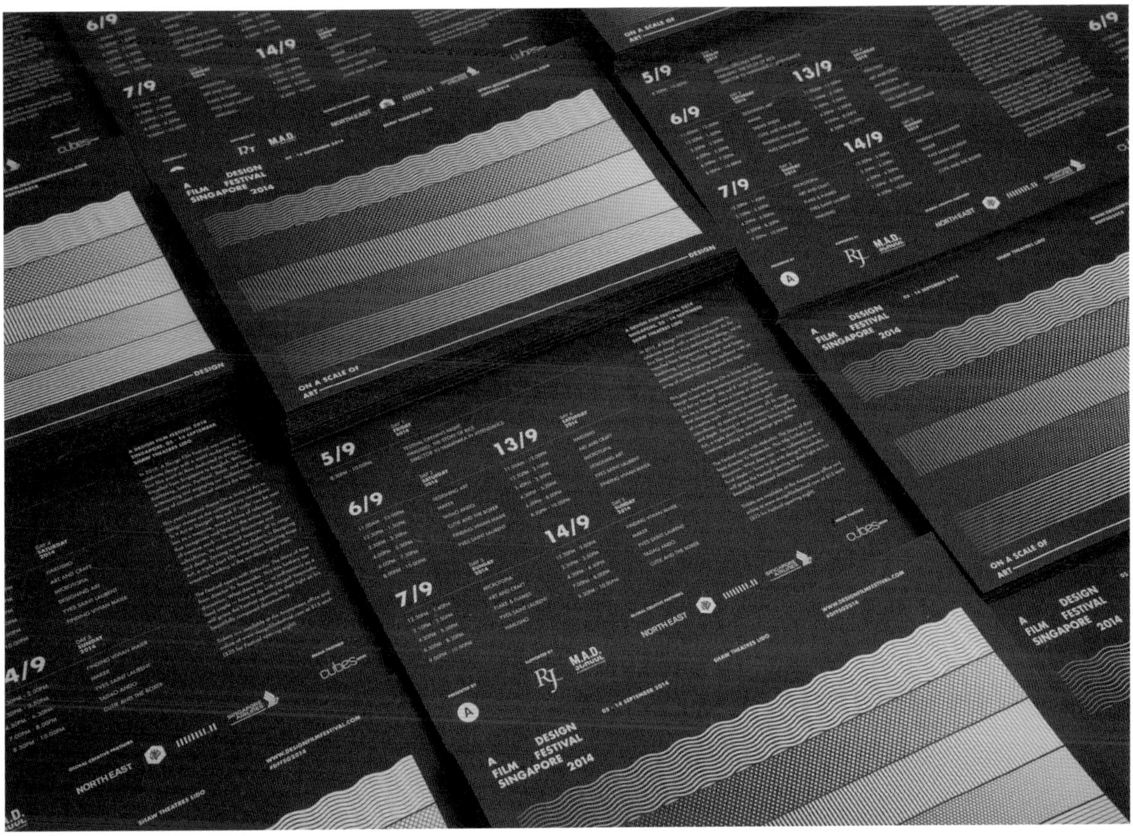

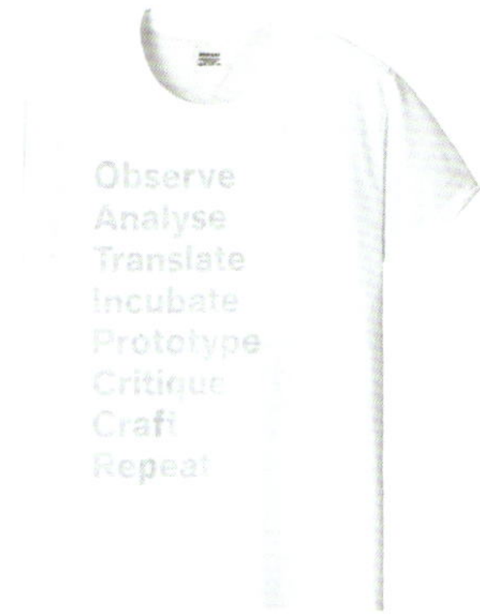
Observe
Analyse
Translate
Incubate
Prototype
Critique
Craft
Repeat

SKY SKY SUN
ROOFTOP
FLOOR
FLOOR
FLOOR
FLOOR
FLOOR
FLOOR
SHADOW
GROUND
BIG TREE

NO
W.

where individuals engage
raw & semi-raw materials
& component parts to
produce, transform, or
reconstruct material
possessions, including
those drawn from the
natural environment.[1]

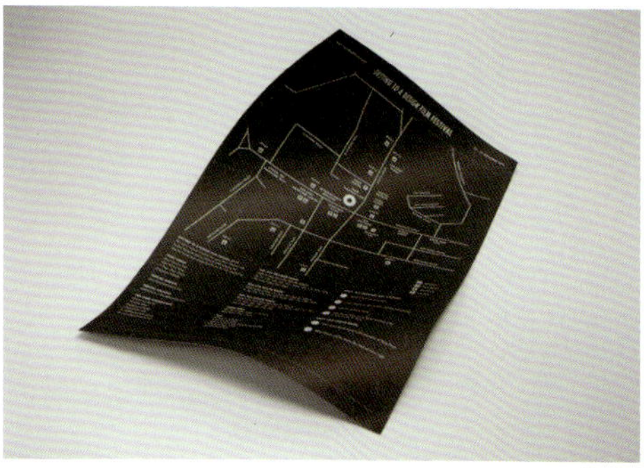

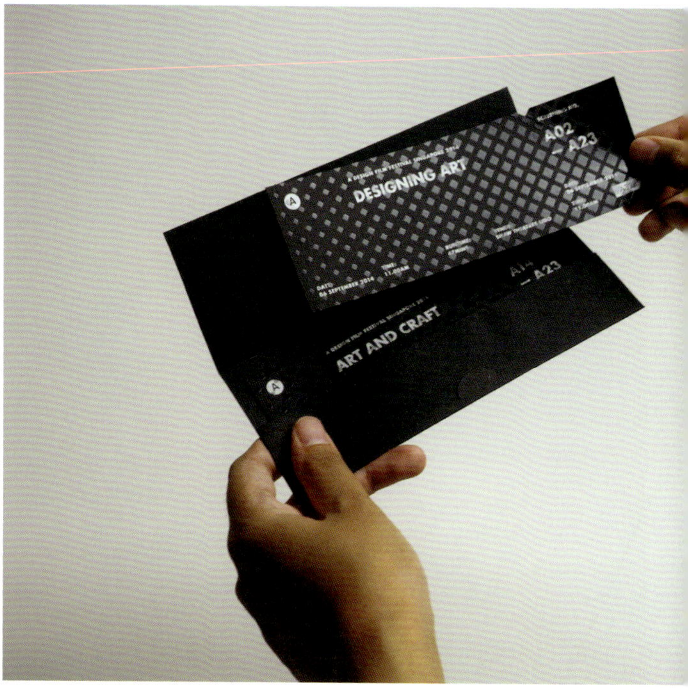
DESIGNING ART
A02
— A23
ART AND CRAFT
A14
— A23

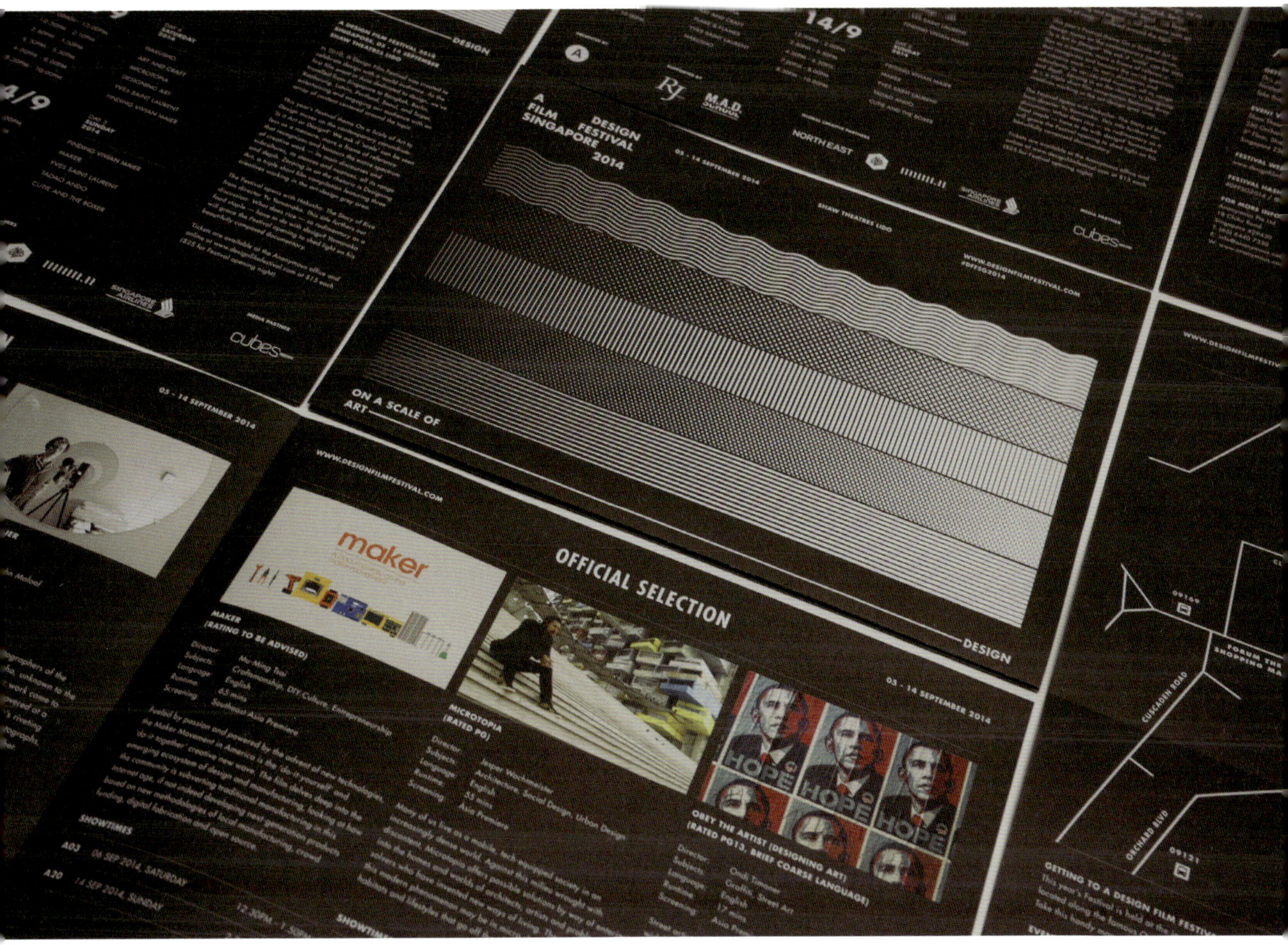
A FILM DESIGN FESTIVAL SINGAPORE 2014
ON A SCALE OF ART
OFFICIAL SELECTION
DESIGN
maker
www.designfilmfestival.com
05 - 14 SEPTEMBER 2014

North East x A Design Film Festival 2014
Special Edition T-shirt Series
The Art of Design
NORTH EAST

De Intuitiëfabriek

—Raw Color

Patterning Biotop paper in laser cut apertures, Raw Color produces a tactile set of business cards, compliment cards and stationery for an all-female industrial design trio, De Intuïtiefabriek. Tangible feel of material delivers the studio's strive for craftsmanship. The collateral is printed in various intensities of a single colour that is visually pure, precise and almost fragile, just like what De Intuïtiefabriek creates.

Client De Intuitiëfabriek
Effects Laser cutting

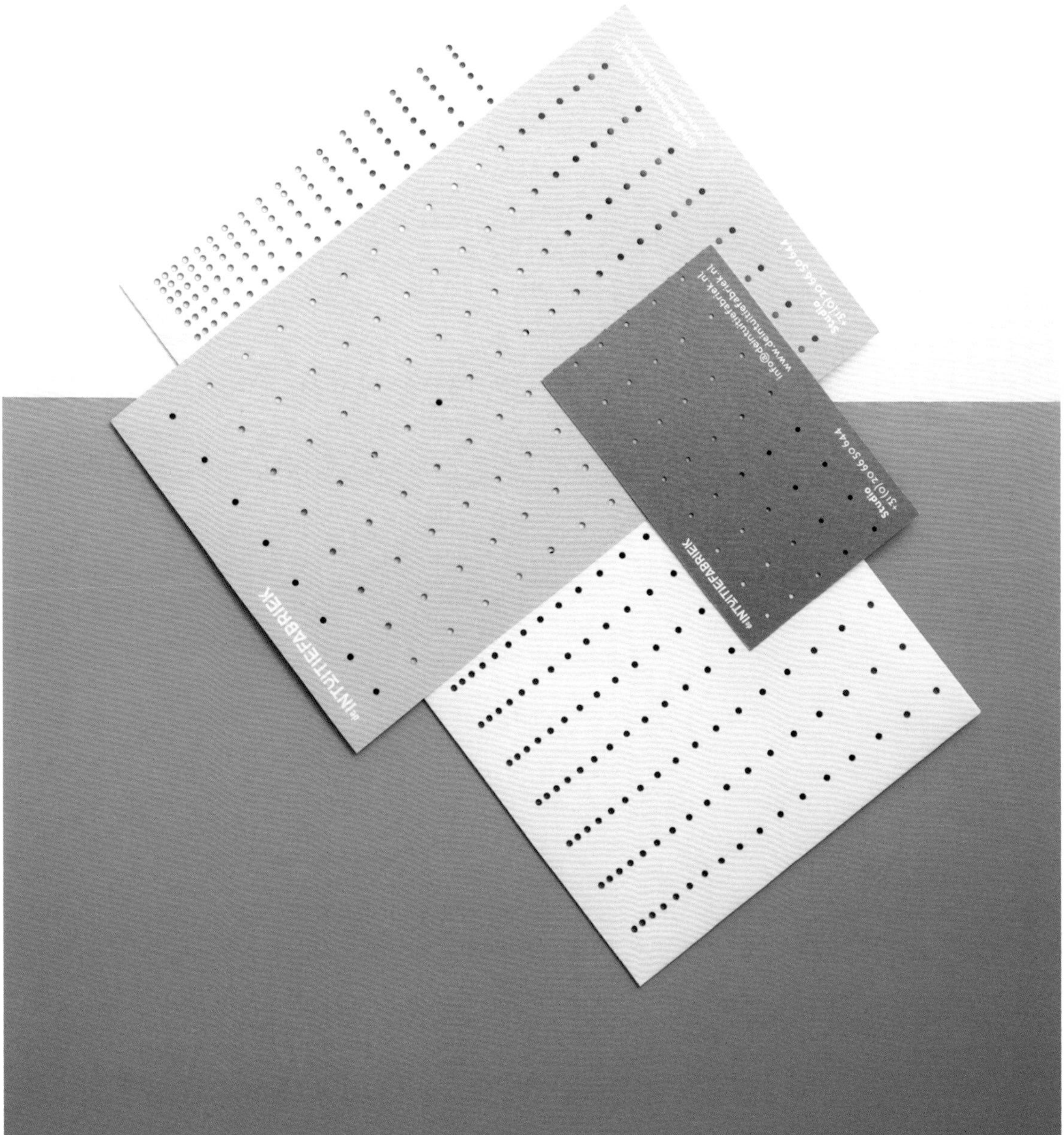

+31 (0) 61 86 81 973
amba@deintuitiefabriek.nl
info@deintuitiefabriek.nl
www.deintuitiefabriek.nl

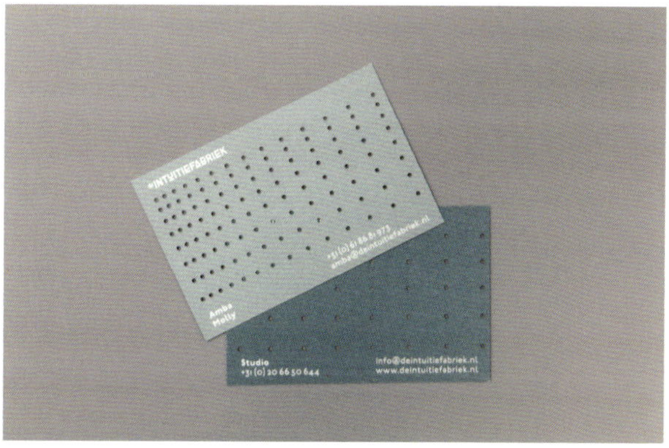
Studio
+31 (0) 30 66 50 644
info@deintuitiefabriek.nl
www.deintuitiefabriek.nl

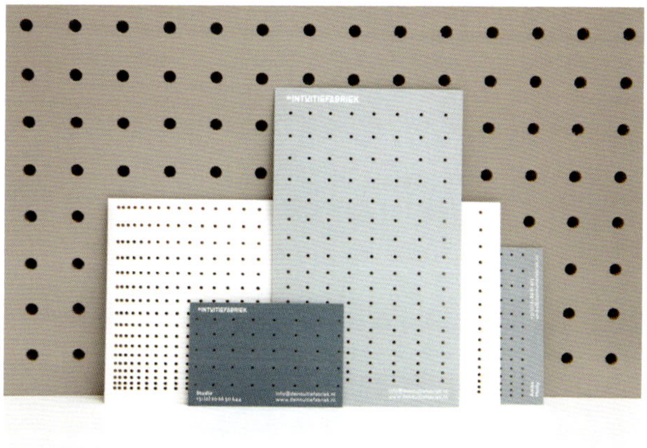

INTUITIEFABRIEK

Jeremy Maxwell Wintrebert Identity

—Hey

The identity for Jeremy Maxwell Wintrebert is designed with a wish to genuinely share with people the practice of modern glass art. Prominent laser-burned patterns offer a glimpse of the glass artist's creative process, even a faint whiff of the wet newspaper that the artist uses to shape the hot glass. Showcards of Wintrebert's free-hand glass blowing works is also designed to materialise the artist's creative spirit conveyed in collateral.

Client Jeremy Maxwell Wintrebert
Photo Roc Canals
Effects Hot stamping, laser cutting

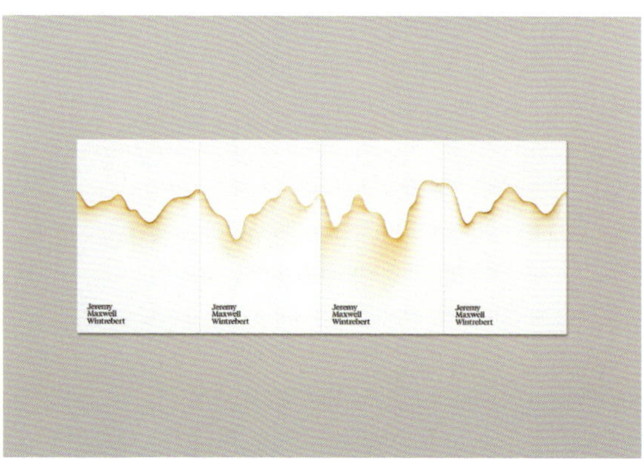

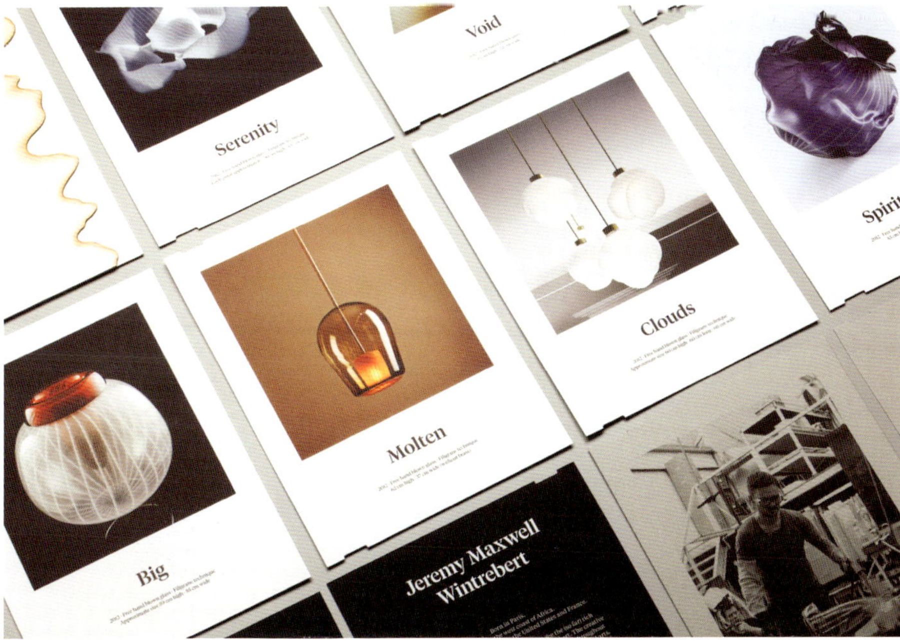
Void
Serenity
Clouds
Molten
Big
Jeremy Maxwell
Wintrebert

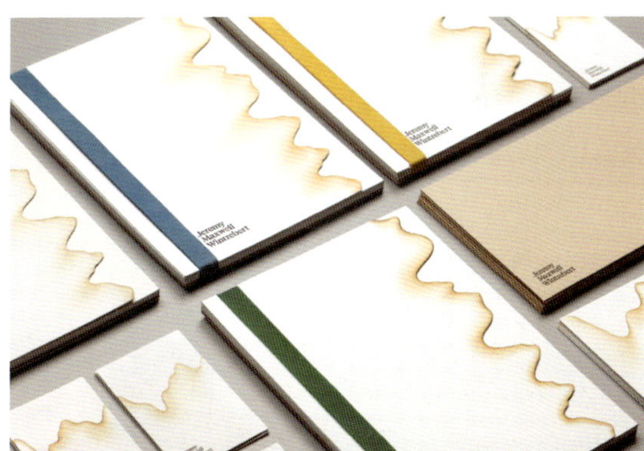

Jeremy
Maxwell
Wintrebert
Jeremy
Maxwell
Wintrebert

Void
2012 - Free hand blown glass
60 cm high - 32 cm wide

Frederik Laux Photography Identity

—ADDA Studio

Reducing to the crossbars of Frederik Laux's initials, a three-strip geometric code is printed on grey chipboards with turquoise tapes diagonally across. Included in the set are letter paper and portfolio pages perforated by hand die-cutter, and business cards printed with letterpress and finished by an edge tipping by hand. The handmade vibe adds individuality to the German photographer's branding solution.

Client Frederik Laux
Effects Die cutting, letterpress, edge dipping

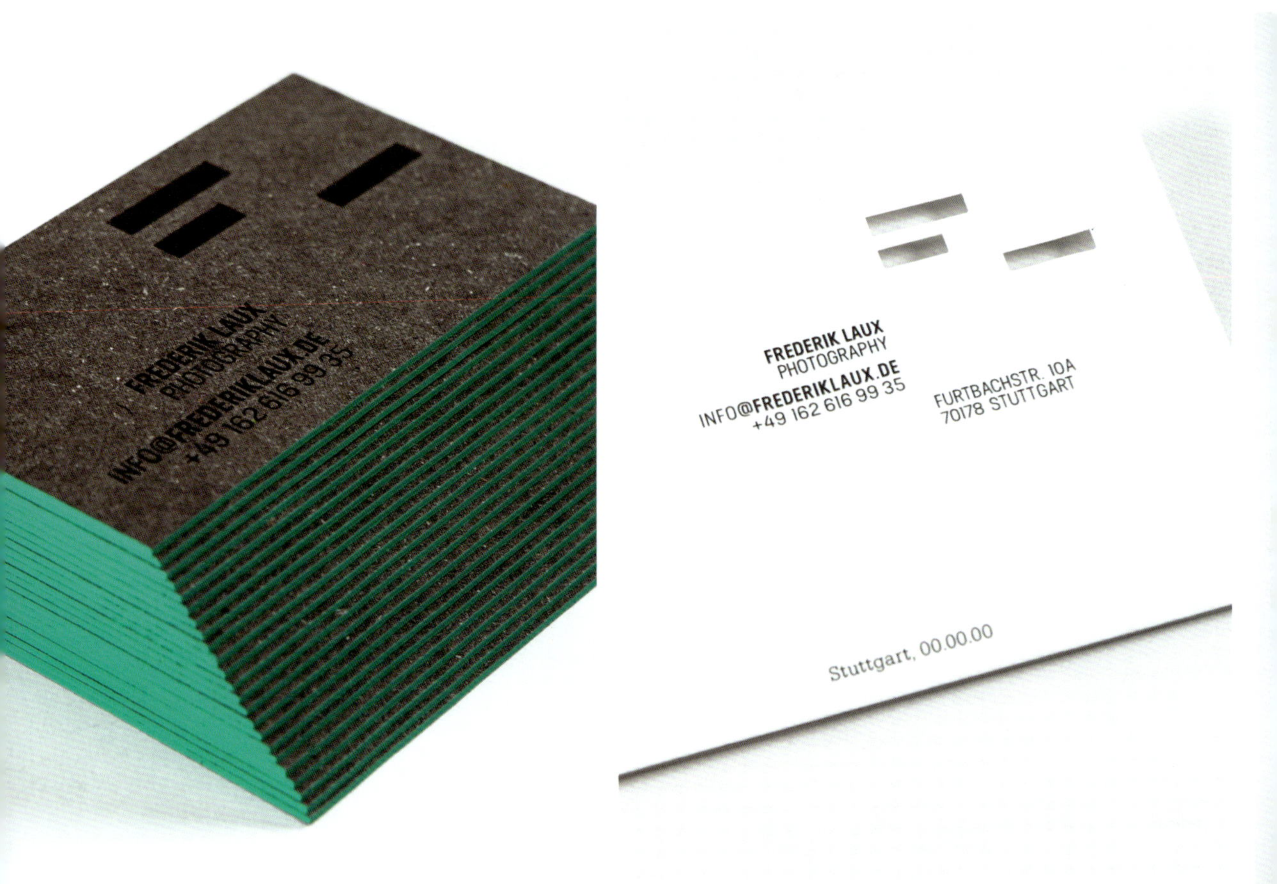

N&P Wedding Invitation

—ADDA Studio

The chemistry of the romantic touch offered by the elegant mint green Gmund paper and the golden foil logotype embossed on raw grey chipboard constitutes a mixed groove of 1960s fusion jazz the soon-to-be-wedded couple adore. Also gold-stamped flowing hand script and black-debossed upper case draws a beautiful contrast throughout invitations, name plates, menus and thank you messages.

Client (not to be disclosed)
Effects Technical folding, hot stamping, debossing

Nora &
Philipp
DANKSAGUNG

Nora &
Philipp
HEIRATEN
Nora &
Philipp
DANKSAGUNG
Nora &
Philipp
MENÜKARTE

Kristina
MUELLER

Alexandra
KRAMMER

World Cup Stamps 2014

—MAAN Design Studio

Excited by the announcement of 20th FIFA World Cup stamps, football lovers and collectors at MAAN Design Studio teamed up to produce a set of stamps that intrigues fans of 32 national teams. The character of the 32 countries are portrayed using a mix of 12 colours. The consistent geometric composition sets a formal context, while lending a visual rhythm of movement for the sport and travelling between these nations.

Effects Die cutting, spot colour

ENGLAND VS ITALY
FOOTBALL WORLD CUP 2014
MATCH 8 | GROUP D
SATURDAY 14 JUN
WORLD CUP
STAMPS
GROUP G
WORLD CUP
STAMPS

GROUP D
URUGUAY | ASOCIACIÓN URUGUAYA DE FÚTBOL
COSTA RICA | FEDERACIÓN COSTARRICENSE DE FÚTBOL
ENGLAND | THE FOOTBALL ASSOCIATION
ITALY | FEDERAZIONE ITALIANA GIUOCO CALCIO
GROUP E
SWITZERLAND | ASSOCIATION SUISSE DE FOOTBALL
ECUADOR | FEDERACIÓN ECUATORIANA DE FÚTBOL
FRANCE | FÉDÉRATION FRANÇAISE DE FOOTBALL
HONDURAS | F. N. AUTÓNOMA DE FÚTBOL DE HONDURAS

WORLD CUP
STAMPS

ALGERIA VS
FOOTBALL WORLD CUP 2014
MATCH 48 | GROUP H
THURSDAY 26 JUN
KICK OFF 17:00 GMT-3
ARENA DA BAIXADA, CURITIBA
STAMPS

WORLD CUP STAMPS

Jammy Yummy

—Hey

Miami-based Jammy Yummy offers a range of all-natural handmade vegetable jams with the ambition of trail-blazing veggie consumption by letting people enjoy their products in simple yet delightful ways. The labels feature a set of random die-cut perforations where random holes symbolise a constant nibbling, an urge induced by food. Colours match the six flavours, including red pepper, baby portobello, jalapeño, caramelised onion and carrot.

Client Jammy Yummy
Photo Roc Canals
Effects Die cutting & perforation

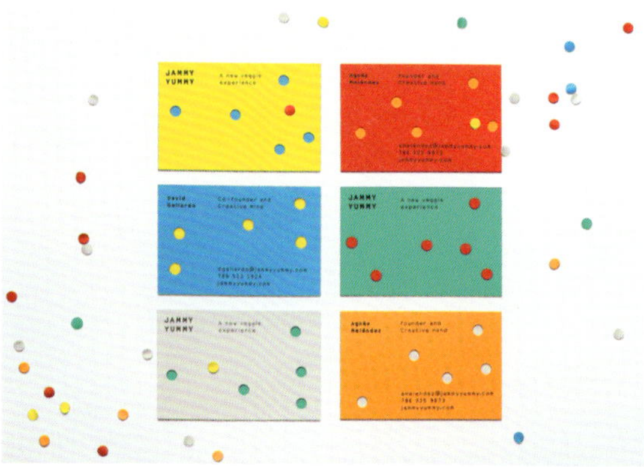

David
Gallardo
Co-founder and
Creative Mind
JAMMY
YUMMY
A new veggie
experience
Agnès
Meléndez
786 925 9873

Google Material Design Printed Kit

—Manual

Material design is Google's approach to a graphic language that can unify their digital platforms and devices under one system. Manual produces a limited edition print kit that interprets the unified visual experience with paper and ink—the physical elements that first inspired the system. Principles of depth effects and movements are communicated in showcards with the help of die cuts, varnish and many more.

Client Google
Effects Die Cutting, technical folding, spot colour, UV varnishing, embossing & debossing

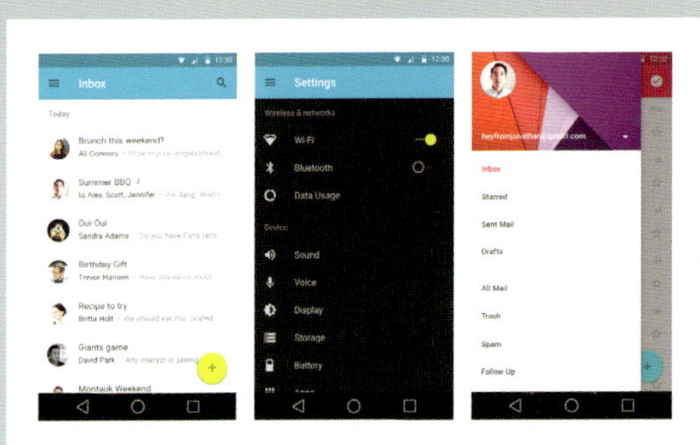

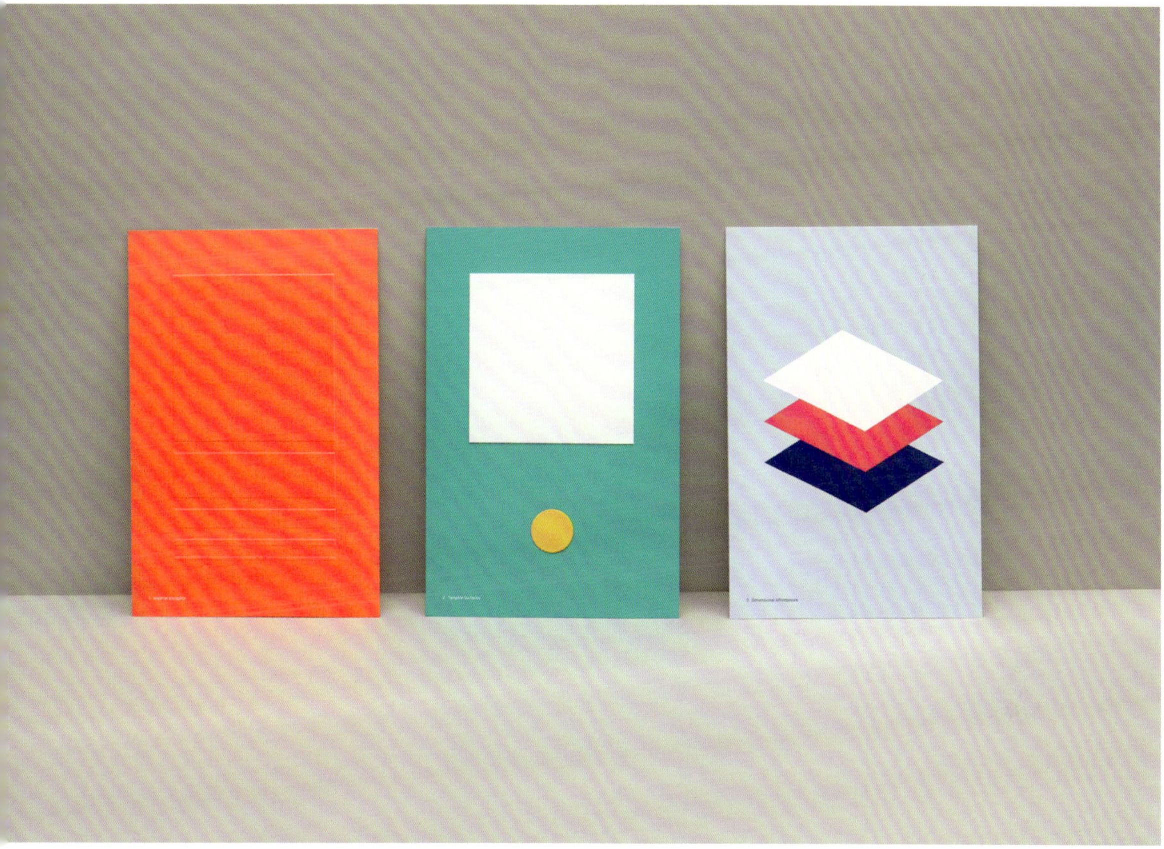

1 Material Metaphor
2 Tangible Surfaces
Material is the metaphor
A material metaphor is the unifying theory of a rationalized space and a system of motion. Our material is grounded in tactile reality, inspired by our study of paper and ink, yet open to imagination and magic.
4 One Design

Design is the art of considered creation. Our goal is to satisfy the diverse spectrum of human needs. As those needs evolve, so too must our designs, practices, and philosophies.
We challenged ourselves to create a visual language for our users that synthesizes the classic principles of good design with the innovation and possibility of technology and science.
This is Material Design
Imagine, Create, Iterate
This is our first step.

3

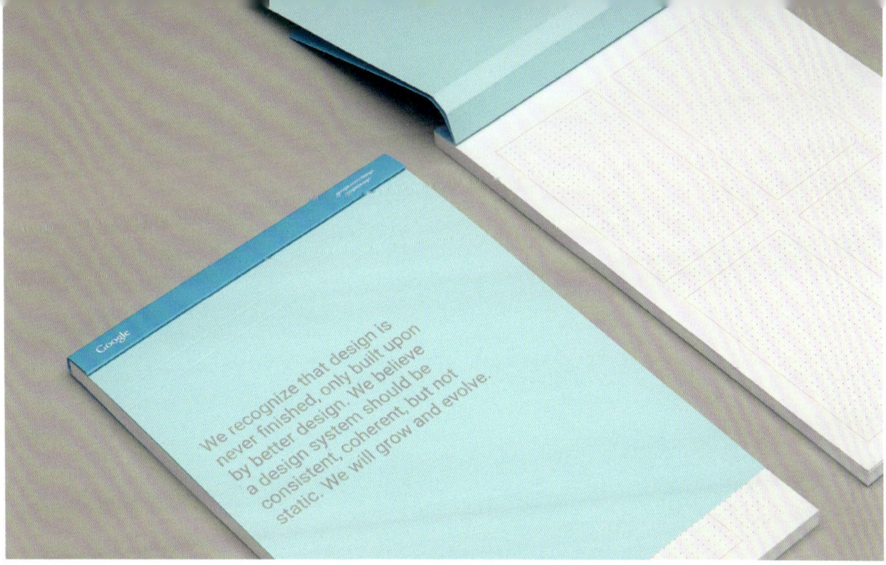
Google
We recognize that design is
never finished, only built upon
by better design. We believe
a design system should be
consistent, coherent, but not
static. We will grow and evolve.

Imagine, Create, Iterate
This is our first step.
This is material design.

Content is bold, graphic,
and intentional
5
Animation is choreographed
on a shared stage

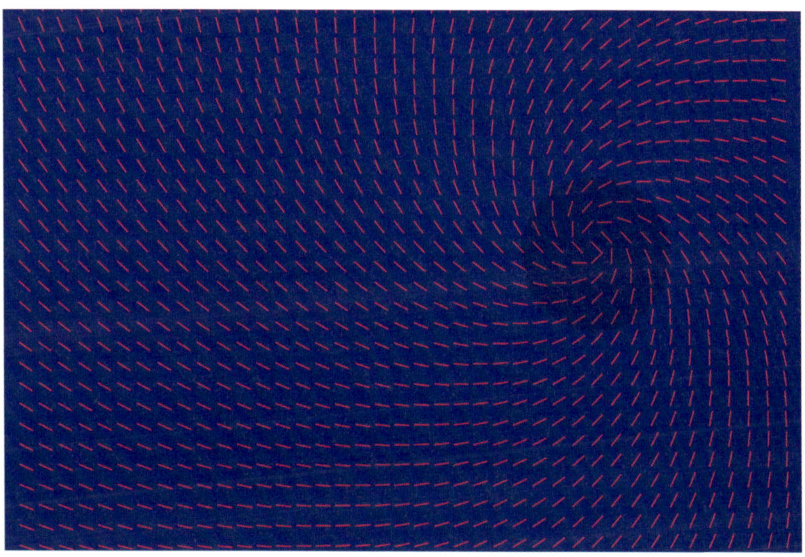

Rendez-vous des créateurs 2014

—MARKS

Rendez-vous des créateurs is a showcase of printing materials and finishing technologies by leading Swiss craftsmen and specialists. Linear and compact, fragments of marker pen script robustly spell out sounds associated with printing, giving the project the apt name of onomatopoeia. Tactile finishes by hot stamping, embossing and flocked type work along with screenprint to capture the expressive nature of the event's theme.

Client Rendez-vous des créateurs
Typography David Zahno (MARKS)
Effects Special ink, hot stamping, embossing, screenprinting, technical binding

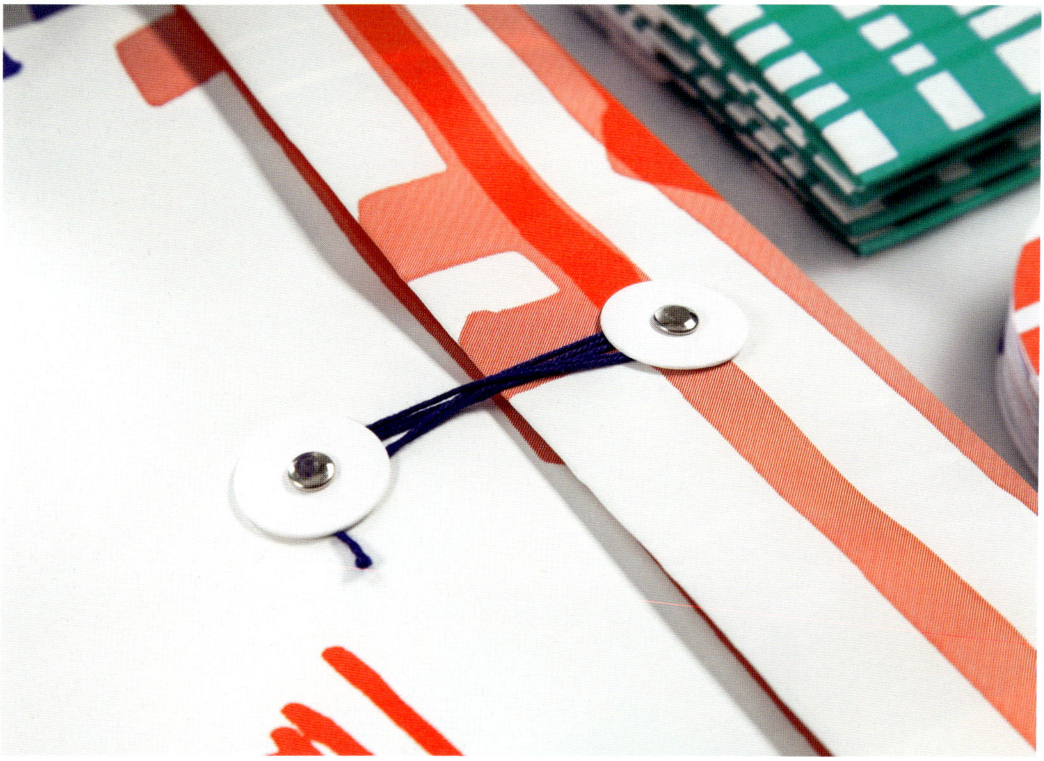

Invitation — Rendez-vous des créateurs
3 et 4 septembre 2014 au Flux Laboratory — Carouge
wwW.rdvcreateurs.ch
Date — 3 et 4 septembre 2014
Lieu — Flux Laboratory
Adresse — Rue Jacques-Dalphin 10, 1227 Carouge (Genève)

Winter
&
Com-
pany

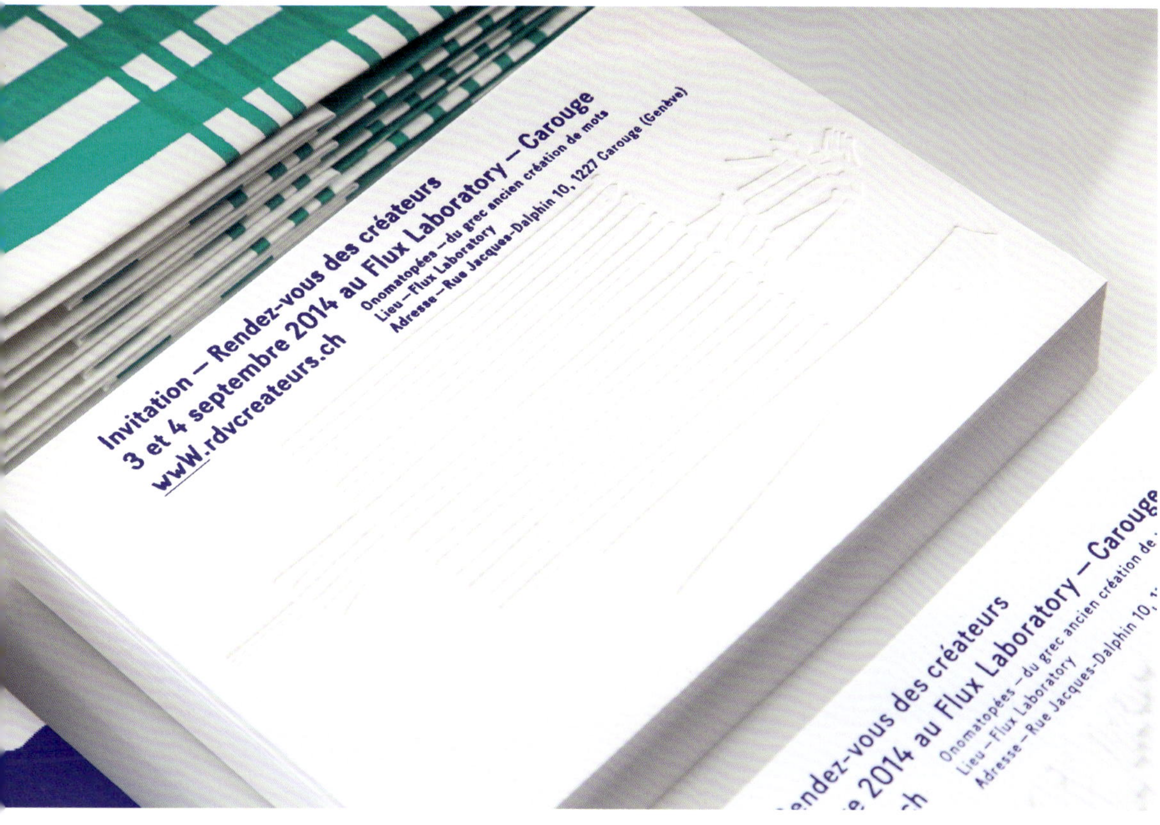
Invitation — Rendez-vous des créateurs
3 et 4 septembre 2014 au Flux Laboratory — Carouge
wwW.rdvcreateurs.ch
Onomatopées — du grec ancien création de mots
Lieu — Flux Laboratory
Adresse — Rue Jacques-Dalphin 10, 1227 Carouge (Genève)

Boreálica Identity

—Anagrama

Boreálica is a clinic for whole body cryotherapy, a treatment that decreases inflammation, pain and enhance cellular survival with low temperatures. To convey a polar sensation, Anagrama has created an austere visual identity using white, grey and holographic foil blocks, that also resonates with the values of health, technology and hygiene—appealing to their target market of professional athletes and health conscious individuals.

Client Boreálica
Effects Die cutting, hot stamping

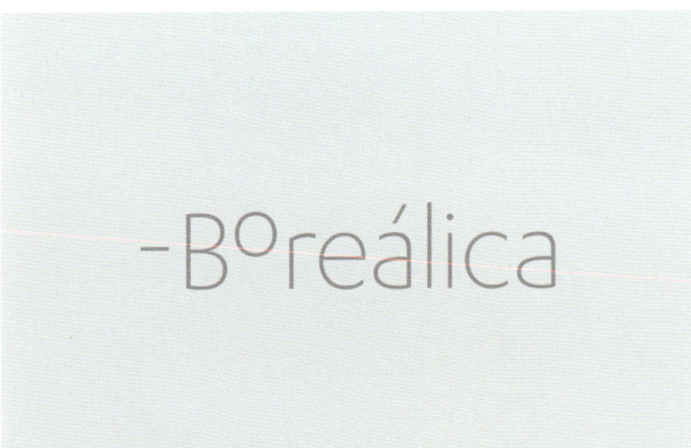

-Boreálica
-Boreálica
-Boreálica

-Bo

-Bo
www.borealica.com
Boreálica es el nombre comercial del
primer studio de crioterapia de cuerpo
entero en la ciudad de Monterrey.

-Bo

-Bo

OTNA Oddds The New Anthropology

—Oddds

Penang and Singapore based creative studio Oddds, use a whimsical collage of pictorial metaphors for their rebrand. Typographically driven, fine graphic detailing and serif type on the collateral is crafted in letterpress, matte gold and copper foils for tactility. Jet black paper creates a mood of secrecy, affirming one of their values that all things imaginable can be created beneath surfaces.

Effects Hot stamping, letterpress

BY ODDDS
The NEW Anthropology
GLAMOUR of ILLUSION
BY CLAIRVOYANCE
MAGIC in FUTURISM
A CERTAIN MYSTIQUE
THAT BRINGS TOGETHER

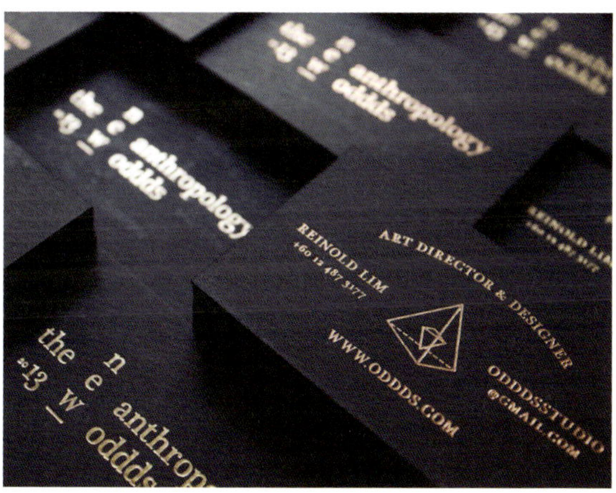
anthropology
odddds
REINOLD LIM
+60 12 487 3177
ART DIRECTOR & DESIGNER
WWW.ODDDS.COM
ODDDSSTUDIO
@GMAIL.COM

HUMBLY SEALED, PACKED
RECIPIENT
anthropology
odddds
WWW.ODDDS.COM

WITH
ALL THINGS
IMAGINABLE
BENEATH SURFACES
ALL GOODS WERE
HANDSOMELY MADE
WITH IMAGINATION &
ACCURACY FOR YOU

ODDDS
the new
anthropology
ODDDS

GBOX Studio Indentity

—Bratus

GBOX is a photography and production studio in Vietnam. Inspired by the bladed aperture of lens, Bratus developed a comprehensive branding solution including a logo, crafted peripherals, and folded stationery items developed from the hexagonal brand mark. A blazing yellow palette and the silhouette of a 3D box is ubiquitous in the array of collateral to address the studio's full name GOLDENBOX.

Client Gbox Studios
Photo Eric Huynh
Effects Die cutting, technical folding, hot stamping, embossing & debossing

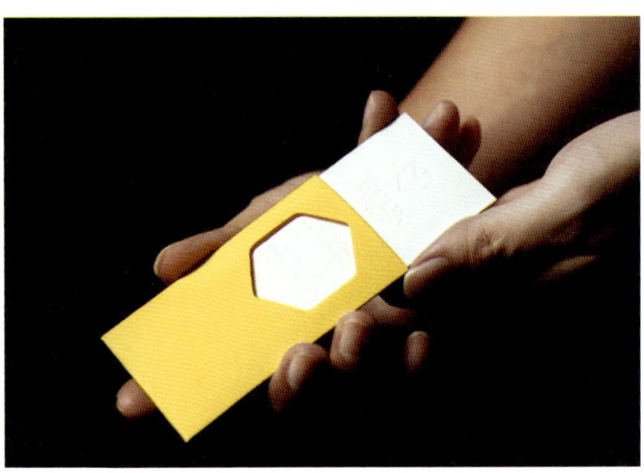

GBOX
EXPLORE CREATE
INSPIRE
G B O X

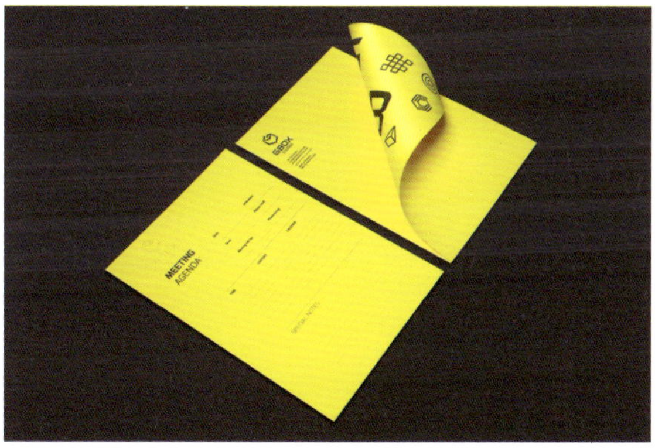
MEETING
AGENDA

GBOX

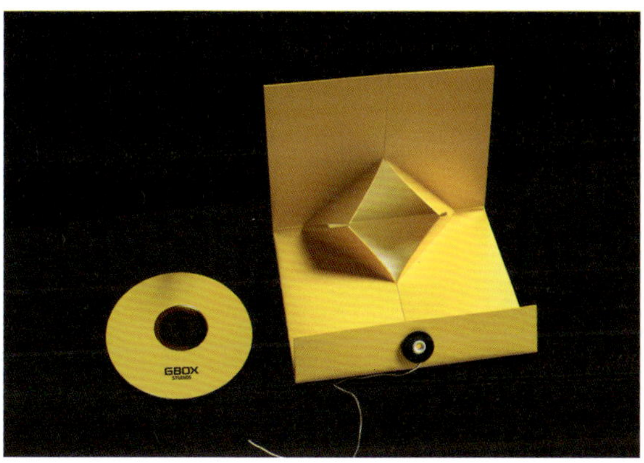
GBOX

A Sculptor's Identity

—Ágnes Herr

Hungarian sculptor Dóra Vanda Demcsák works mainly with metals and her identity was designed to reflect this. Printed on and wrapped in aluminium sheets, the lucent array of deliverables is marked with a reduced logotype from her initials. Utilising the malleability of the material, one can create a sculpture out of her business cards and her "Horses" exhibition flyers, as a tribute to the sculpture's craft of creasing and creating still life out of a sheet.

Client Dóra Vanda Demcsák
Effects Technical folding, non-paper materials

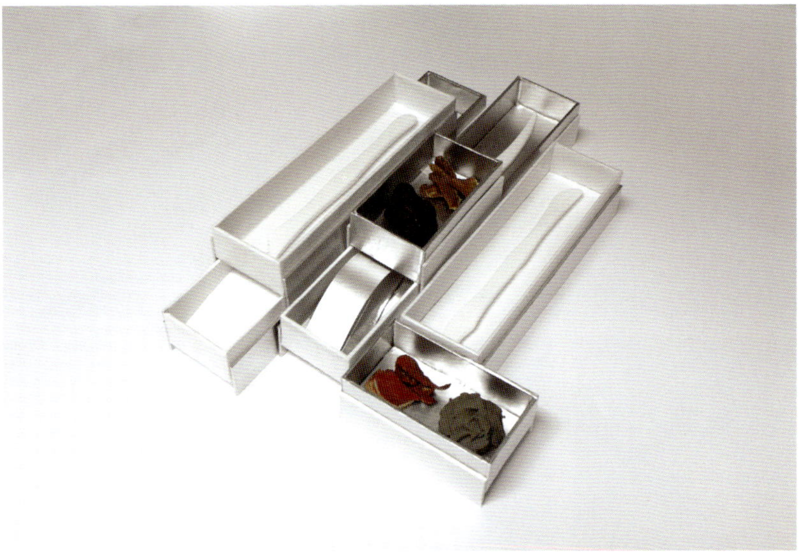

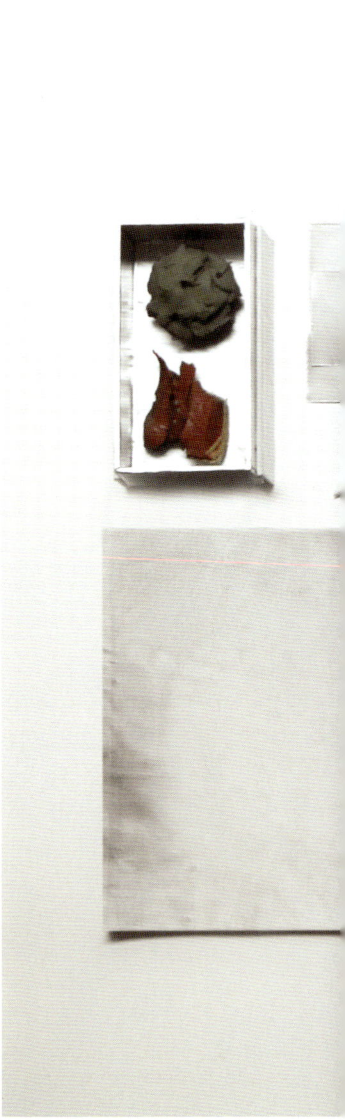

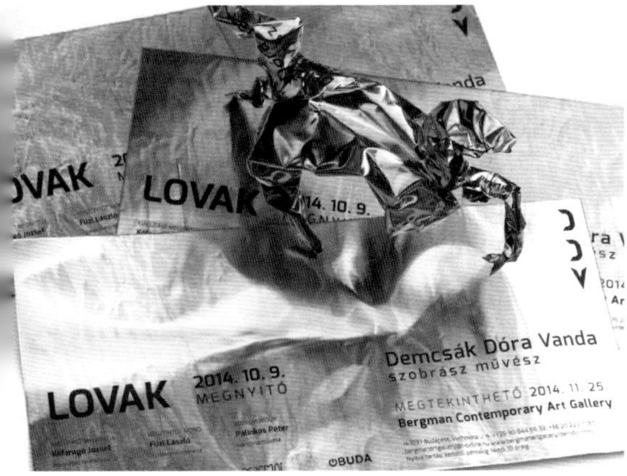
LOVAK
2014. 10. 9.
MEGNYITÓ
Demcsák Dóra Vanda
szobrász művész
MEGTEKINTHETŐ 2014. 11. 25.
Bergman Contemporary Art Gallery
ÓBUDA

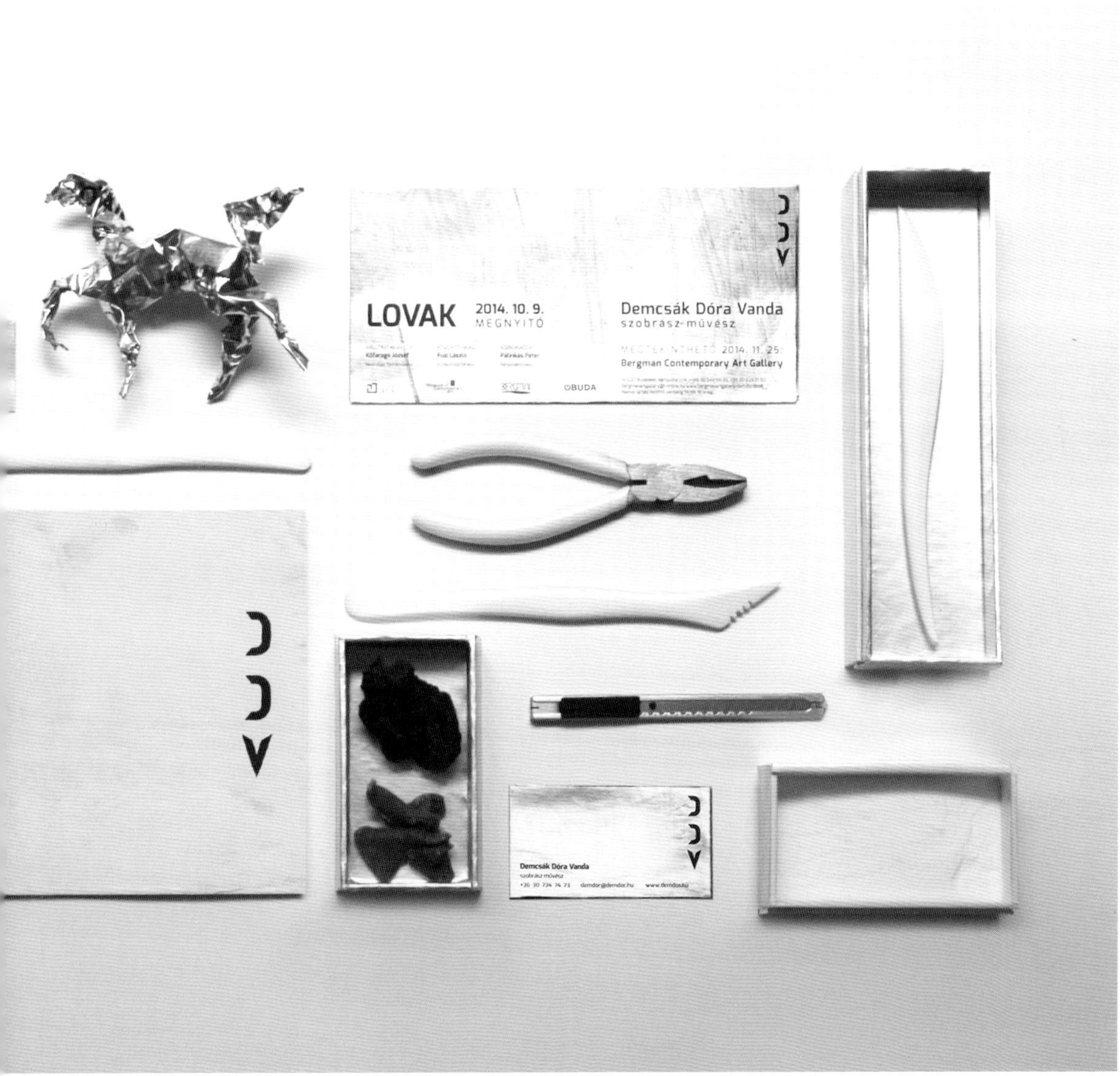
LOVAK
2014. 10. 9.
MEGNYITÓ
Demcsák Dóra Vanda
szobrász-művész
MEGTEKINTHETŐ 2014. 11. 25.
Bergman Contemporary Art Gallery
ÓBUDA
Demcsák Dóra Vanda

CUTTER ART of OLFA

—DENTSU INC.

Cutting tool specialist OLFA wanted to accentuate the precision and ability of its knives. The team behind the campaign spent a whole year snipping and stacking foam boards and paper to create an array of geometric patterns that is huge in scale yet intricately detailed. Overhead shots and isometric projections of the models were shot to highlight the brand in the posters and other corporate items such as business cards.

Client OLFA
Effects Die cutting

OLFA
CUTTER
ART OF
OLFA 2011
EXHIBITION
@b+f
4.01 [FRI]-4.24 [SUN] 13:00-19:00
OPENING PARTY 4.01 [FRI] 19:00-21:00

OLFA
オルファ株式会社 http://www.olfa.co.jp

OLFA
オルファ株式会社 http://www.olfa.co.jp

OLFA
オルファ株式会社 http://www.olfa.co.j

GRYPS — Prison Poetry Festival

— Zuzanna Rogatty

"Gryps" is a polish word that refers to the secret messages that get passed in and out of prison. It is also suitably the name of Prison Poetry Festival. Featuring objects found in prison, flyers were folded into paper planes, a symbol of transience and a reminder of the longing for freedom, but were then crushed to fortify a sense of despair. A slight gloominess was conveyed through the collateral, which was printed in greyscale on low quality paper with a lopsided logo.

Effects Technical folding, technical binding

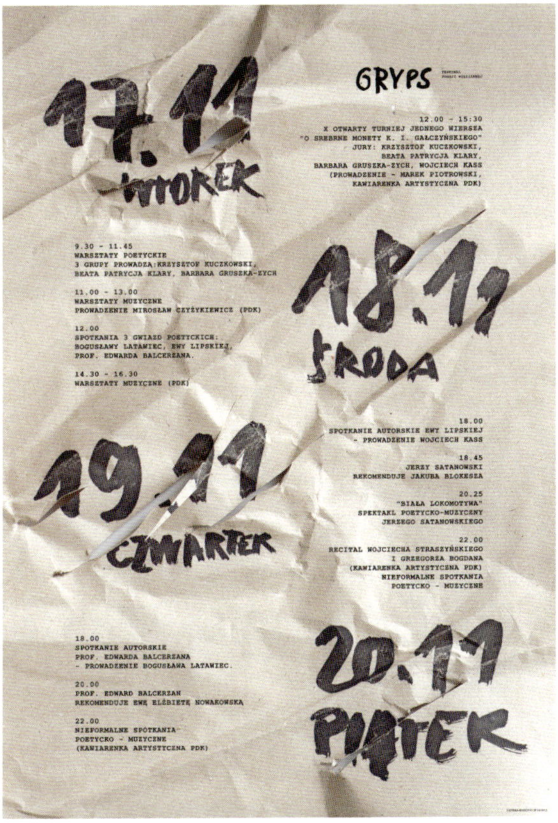
GRYPS
12.00 - 15:30
X OTWARTY TURNIEJ JEDNEGO WIERSZA
"O SREBRNE MONETY K. I. GAŁCZYŃSKIEGO"
JURY: KRZYSZTOF KUCZKOWSKI,
BEATA PATRYCJA KLARY,
BARBARA GRUSZKA-ZYCH, WOJCIECH KASS
(PROWADZENIE - MAREK PIOTROWSKI,
KAWIARENKA ARTYSTYCZNA PDK)
17.11
WTOREK
9.30 - 11.45
WARSZTATY POETYCKIE
3 GRUPY PROWADZĄ:KRZYSZTOF KUCZKOWSKI,
BEATA PATRYCJA KLARY, BARBARA GRUSZKA-ZYCH
11.00 - 13.00
WARSZTATY MUZYCZNE
PROWADZENIE MIROSŁAW CZYŻYKIEWICZ (PDK)
12.00
SPOTKANIA 3 GWIAZD POETYCKICH:
BOGUSŁAWY LATAWIEC, EWY LIPSKIEJ,
PROF. EDWARDA BALCERZANA.
14.30 - 16.30
WARSZTATY MUZYCZNE (PDK)
18.11
ŚRODA
18.00
SPOTKANIE AUTORSKIE EWY LIPSKIEJ
- PROWADZENIE WOJCIECH KASS
18.45
JERZY SATANOWSKI
REKOMENDUJE JAKUBA BLOKESZA
20.25
"BIAŁA LOKOMOTYWA"
SPEKTAKL POETYCKO-MUZYCZNY
JERZEGO SATANOWSKIEGO
22.00
RECITAL WOJCIECHA STRASZYŃSKIEGO
I GRZEGORZA BOGDANA
(KAWIARENKA ARTYSTYCZNA PDK)
NIEFORMALNE SPOTKANIA
POETYCKO - MUZYCZNE
19.11
CZWARTEK
18.00
SPOTKANIE AUTORSKIE
PROF. EDWARDA BALCERZANA
- PROWADZENIE BOGUSŁAWA LATAWIEC.
20.00
PROF. EDWARD BALCERZAN
REKOMENDUJE EWĘ ELŻBIETĘ NOWAKOWSKĄ
22.00
NIEFORMALNE SPOTKANIA
POETYCKO - MUZYCZNE
(KAWIARENKA ARTYSTYCZNA PDK)
20.11
PIĄTEK

FESTIWAL
POEZJI WIEZIENNEJ
17-20.11.2013
ARESZT ŚLEDCZY
W TORUNIU
GRYPS

Darryl Jingwen Wee Business Cards

—Foreign Policy Design Group

The business cards of Japan-based writer, translator and interpreter Darryl Jingwen Wee bring meaning through the use of transference. Transference is a process where information is reiterated from one medium to another every time the contact details are hand-printed onto each card with a transfer marker. Card stock is handmade from Wee's published articles, imbuing the essence of his craft while idiosyncratic by sight and touch.

Client Darryl Jingwen Wee, Japan
Craft May Lim
Effects Technical printing

東京都杉並区阿佐谷北3-3-20
aya Kita, Suginami-ku,
0 6659 1741
8435 0230

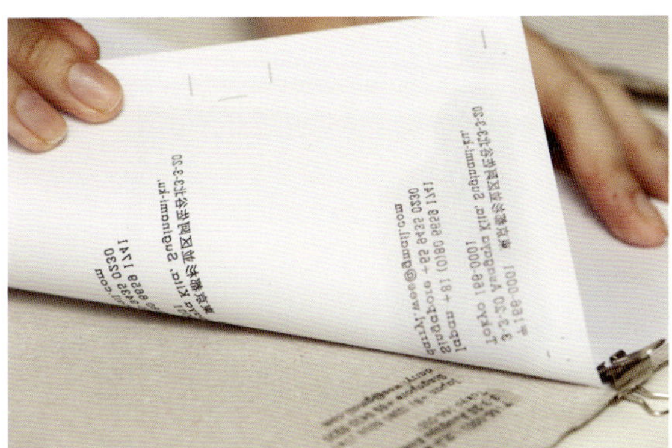

Foreign Policy Moving Announcement Card

—Foreign Policy Design Group

Using materials found right from their new studio site, Foreign Policy's relocation announcements avoid the "we've moved" announcements cliché. A simple tone-on-tone print with tiles that are diagonally split in half on gypsum boards, which meant welcoming their new work space by literally crossing out the old one. The message boards were bubble-wrapped while they were sent off to clients and associates.

Photo Jovian Lim
Effects Screenprinting, non-paper materials

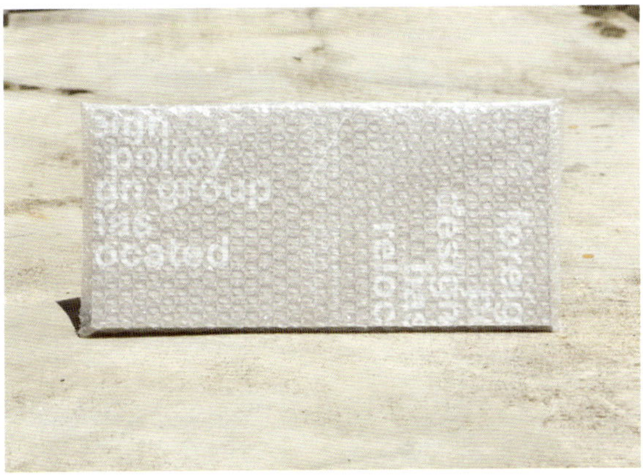

foreig
design
has
reloc

design
has
reloc
number 231a
south bridge road
singapore 058780
78 yong siak street
unit 01-04
singapore 163078

The Folks Studio Identity

—The Folks Studio

Derived of traditional colours, The Folks Studio has built an identity with modernised cultural icons that reflect their Chinese lineage in multi-cultural Singapore. Meaning "people", the Chinese character of "folk" repeats into a monogram that blind embossed on name cards in special paper that allows light through the way old Chinese windows did. The CD holder is a replica of blossoming lotus, a Chinese symbol of nobility.

Effects Die cutting, technical folding, hot stamping

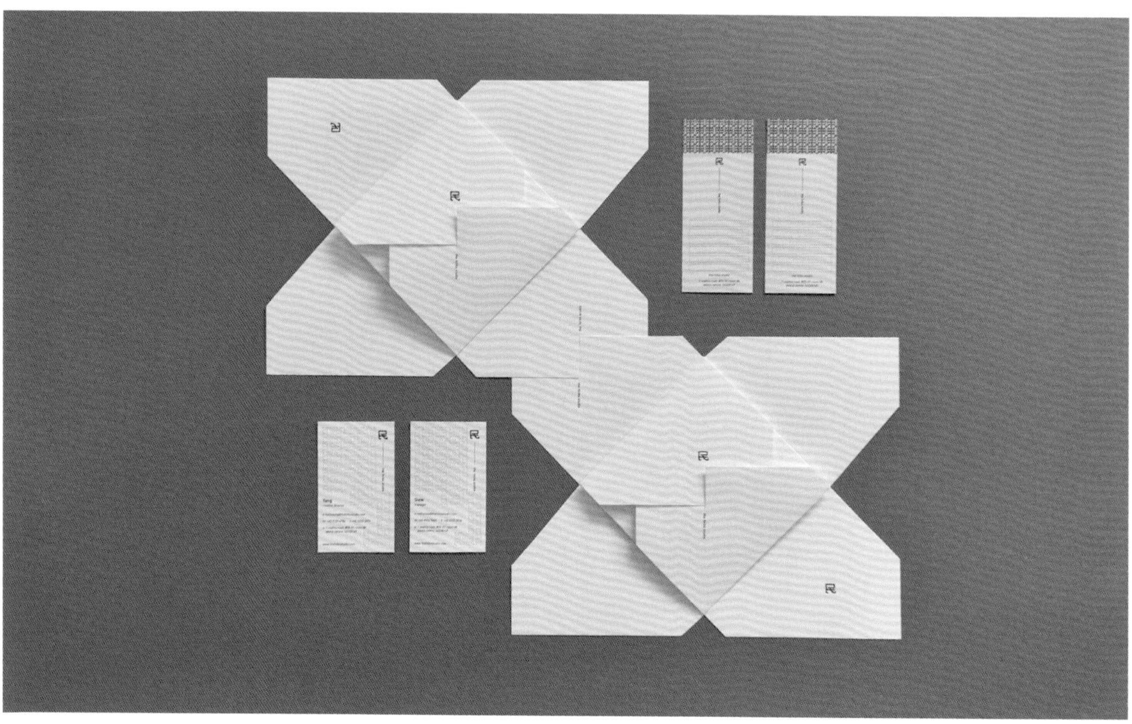

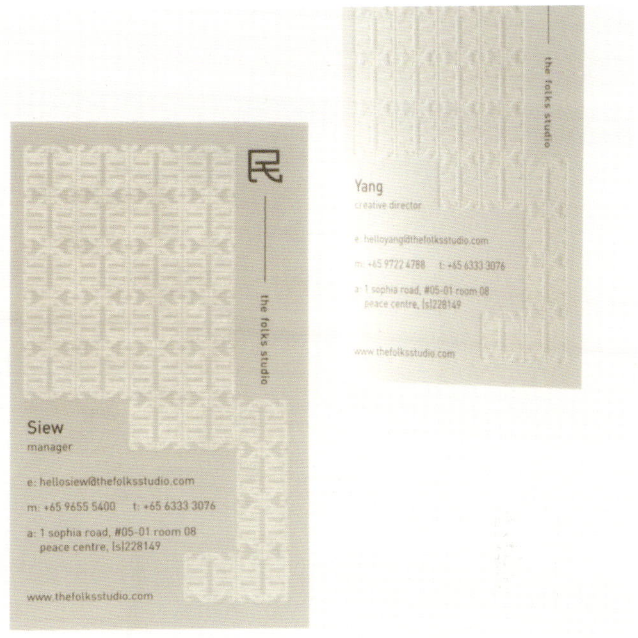

the folks studio
Yang
creative director
e: helloyang@thefolksstudio.com
m: +65 9722 4788 t: +65 6333 3076
a: 1 sophia road, #05-01 room 08
peace centre, [s]228149
www.thefolksstudio.com
the folks studio
Siew
manager
e: hellosiew@thefolksstudio.com
m: +65 9655 5400 t: +65 6333 3076
a: 1 sophia road, #05-01 room 08
peace centre, [s]228149
www.thefolksstudio.com

the folks studio

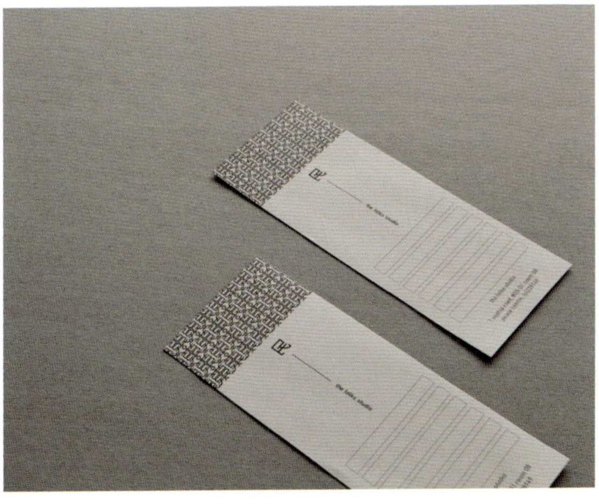

Books & Pages
Books & Pages
Books & Pages
Books & Pages
Books & Pages
Books & Pages
Books & Pages
Books & Pages

The Bowl of Enlightenment

— mistroom

For 'The Bowl of Enlightenment', the team at mistroom played with materiality, where the copper pieces were exposed to the natural environment to absorb sunlight, air, water, sound and time before being put into the book. Through the pages, readers would see the copper piece gradually growing through the expanding die-cut area, which symbolises the resonance of sound; the ripples of waves; and the silent entrance to the Sun, the Earth, and the universe that nourishes us.

Client vima house
Effects Die cutting & perforation, hot stamping, embossing & debossing, non-paper materials

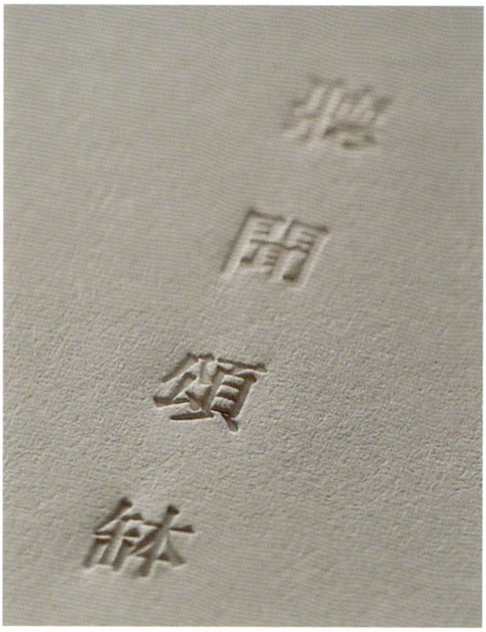

Lukas/Markus by Kalle Sanner

— Lundgren+Lindqvist

'Lukas/Markus' is the outcome of a decade-long photography project by Kalle Sanner, who felt an immediate connection to the Saint Lukas and Saint Markus chapels in Gothenburg by architect Sven Brolid. With printing details and papers that mirror their iconic facades and interior features including a clothbound hardcover embossed with partial transparent foil, double foldouts and a turquoise silk bookmark, the book depicts sensitive portraits of the buildings and their surroundings.

Client Kalle Sanner
Photography Carl Ander
Printing Göteborgstryckeriet
Publishing Il'Editions, Blackbook Publications
Effects Hot stamping, embossing & debossing, non-paper materials

Freies Theater Hannover

— Bureau Hardy Seiler

Freies Theater Hannover offers a diverse programme of classical and contemporary theatre, multimedia productions, musical experiments, modern dance and educational initiatives. Inspired by its logo, Bureau Hardy Seiler designed a publication featuring two ribbons bound with a diagonal cutout on its cover. Inside, information about the different programmes was displayed on separate cards, with the first card made out of different Pantone colours, papers and structures combined.

Client Kulturbüro der Landeshauptstadt Hannover
Printing & Production Letterjazz, Essen
Effects Die cutting & perforation, spot colour, hot stamping, embossing & debossing, letterpress, laser cutting, technical binding

UNVERGLEICHLICH
UNGLEICH
FREIES
THEATER
HANNOVER

12'13, — 01'14
SPIELPLAN
FREIES
THEATER
HANNOVER

12'13, — 01'14
SPIELPLAN
FREIES
THEATER
HANNOVER

Notebook 2

—Anagrama

The technical language of printing production and the concept of technology and computer hardware merge in this book, a collaborative project initiated by Parisian printer Imprimerie du Marais that aims to celebrate special printing effects and techniques. Anagrama exploited extremes, letting colours, shapes and lines dance on Arjowiggins Creative Papers in a pattern inspired by motherboard. Both the content and the production process are a tribute to the complexity and technicality of the printing process as a dying art.

Client Imprimerie du Marais
Effects Hot stamping, embossing & debossing, screenprinting, technical binding

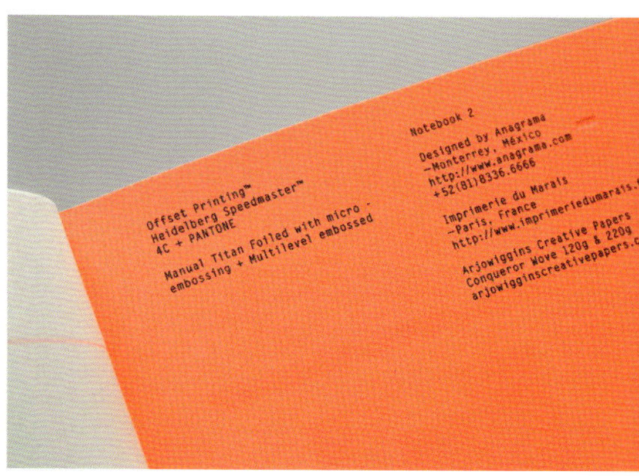

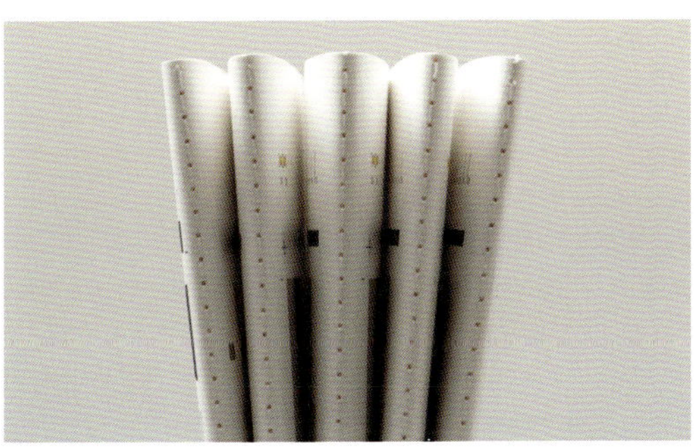

NOTEBOOK
II

U67
Druck/h J.P.H.
2100
R
7
0
R
5
6

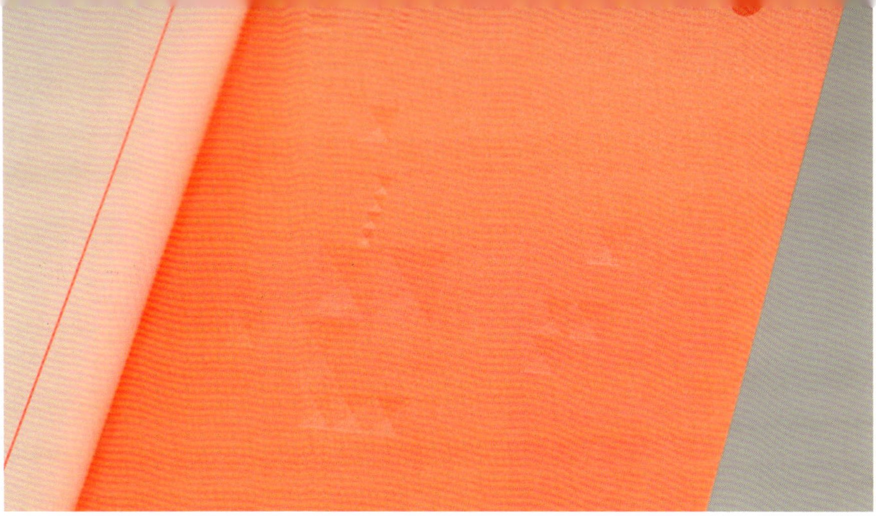

Welcome,
This is Notebook 2
Designed by Anagrama.com

U67
Druck/h J.P.H.
2100

P. S.–Secrets of the Barguzin Skeleton

—Marton Borzak

This book is about the discovery of a skeleton in Siberia, possibly belonging to the great Hungarian poet Sándor Petőfi, whose life was marked with secrecy and mysteries. Related events and documents are told in three layers, mixing actual stories, articles from the time of discovery and sealed messages that were inspired by spy stories. Secret messages are printed with a UV ink and can only be revealed with a UV light attached in the book.

Client BT-Press
Printing Gyomapress
Effects Spot colour, special ink, technical binding

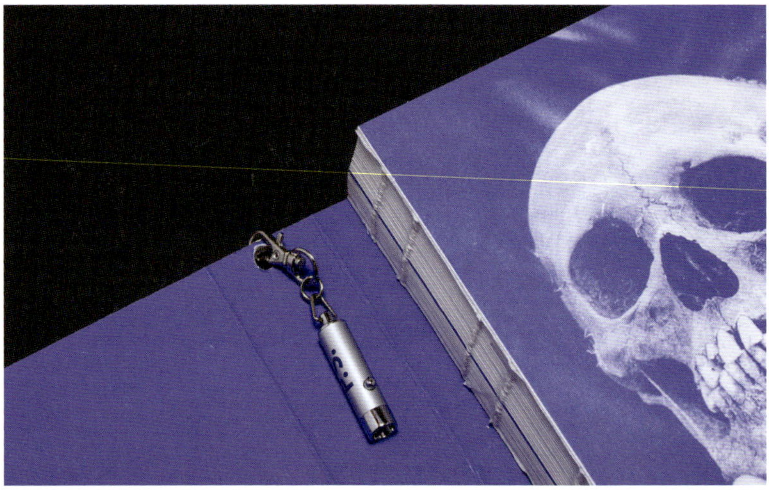

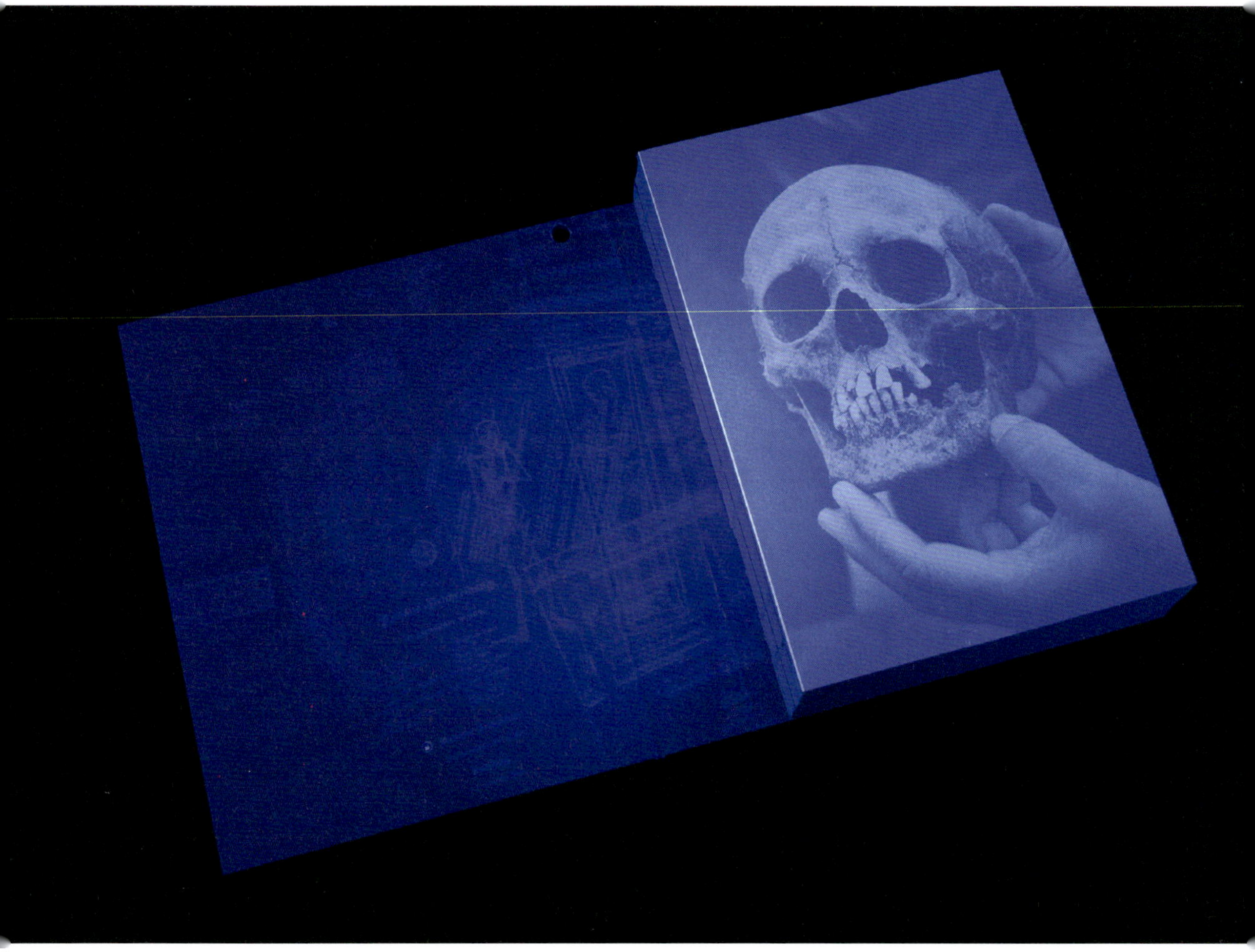

P.S.

P.S.
Titkok a barguzini csontváz körül
BORZÁK TIBOR

P.S.

Sticky Notes Annual

—LENS ASSOCIATES INC.

Addressing the diligence of note-taking amongst Japanese designers, the 2012 Advertising Annual of Copywriters Club Nagoya provides designers the perfect tool to engage with its content without damaging the pages. In stripes or checkers, bespoke sticky notes are affixed on the cover, allowing the owner to mark their favourite projects recognised by the 2012 CCN Award. A list of the award winners unfold themselves as all sticky notes were removed.

Client Copywriters Club Nagoya
Effects Hot stamping

ANNUAL 2012
Club Nagoya

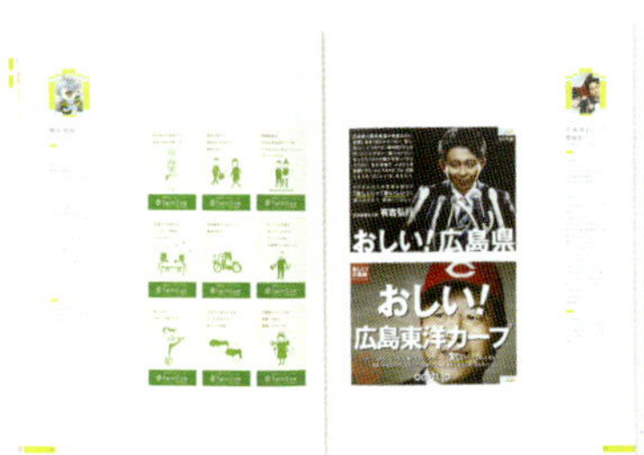
おしい!広島県
おしい!広島東洋カープ

JOIN
2012 CCN AWARD SPECIAL PRIZE
Tomohiko Kawanishi
2012 CCN AWARD RADIO COMMERCIAL
Taizo Hirose
2012 CCN AWARD RADIO COMMERCIAL
Toru Tsuzuki
2012 CCN AWARD GRAPHIC
Kotaro Abe
2012 CCN AWARD GRAPHIC
Masashi Kita, Kenichi Wakita, Hisaya Nagahama
2012 CCN AWARD GRAPHIC
Tomohiko Kawanishi, Shinnosuke Togawa
2012 CCN AWARD GRAPHIC
Osamu Kawaguchi
2012 CCN AWARD GRAPHIC
Yoshiki Toya
2012 CCN AWARD GRAPHIC
Tomoaki Kubota
2013 CCN AWARD WINNER
will surely be you!
ADVERTISING ANNUAL 2012
Copywriters Club Nagoya

Mother Book

—DENTSU INC. CHUBU

This unique book for expecting mothers has 40 pages, each representing a week in the pregnancy process. Information on that particular week of the pregnancy and blank spaces are available for moms-to-be to note down their status and mood, allowing them to have a better understanding of their pregnancy term. With the help of a cutting plotter, the pages literally grow in size and get bigger as time goes on like a baby bump.

Client Bell-net Obstetrics
Special credits LENS ASSOCIATES inc., KITO PRINTING Co.,LTD, Itoubigeisha seihanjo Co.,LTD, AZLINK.,LTD, C3 Film Co.,LTD
Effects Technical cutting

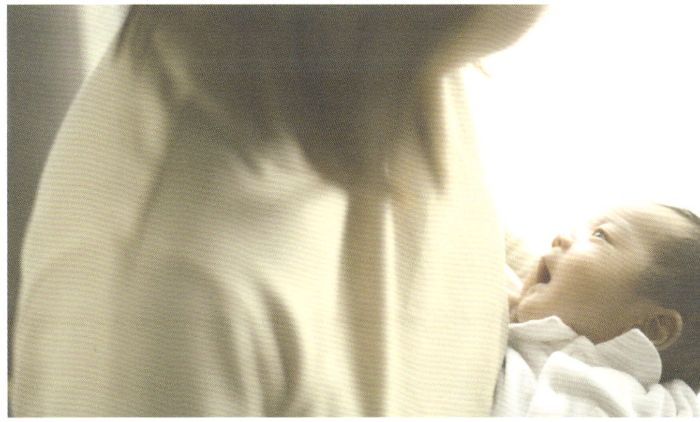

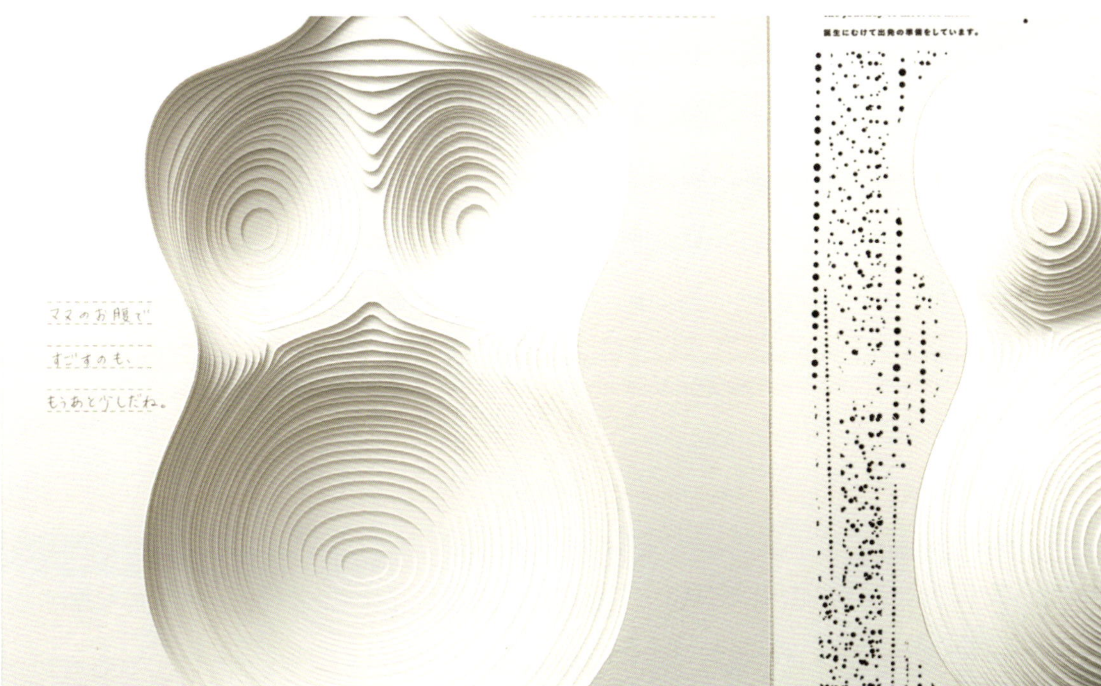
ママのお腹で
すごすのも、
もうあと少しだね。
誕生にむけて出発の準備をしています。

1

4

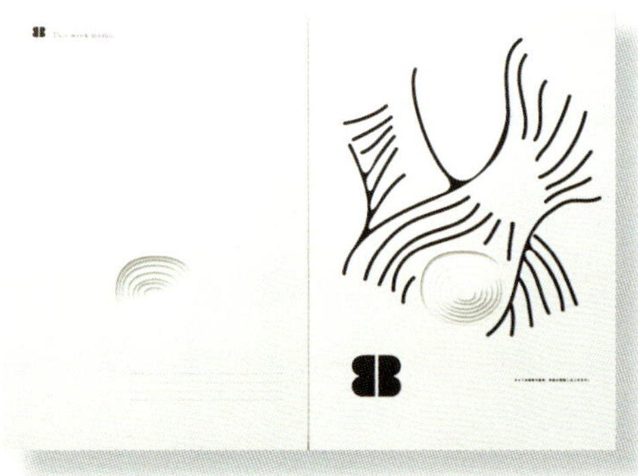

10

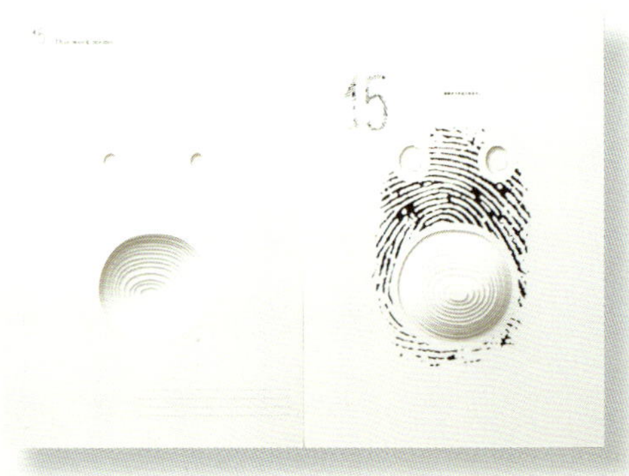
15

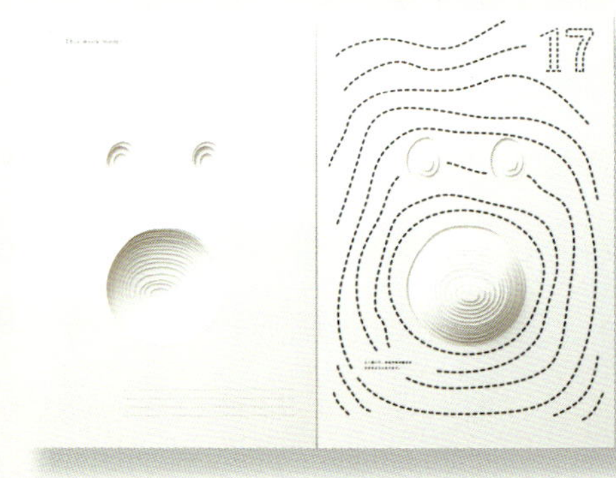
17

18
こんにちは。Сайнбайна
Ciao kaixo
SALUTON Hello
ahoj
CHÀO
Hallå
Bonjour
18 हॅलो
Habari
你好
salve
Alo
Olá
Habari
Алло
NDEWO
Hola
Hola sveiki
안녕하세요
Pozdravljeni
Γειασας გამარჯობა

20
Aku mencintaimu
AKU MENCINTAIMU
Jagälskar
Ich liebe dich
I LOVE YOU.
Jeg elsker deg

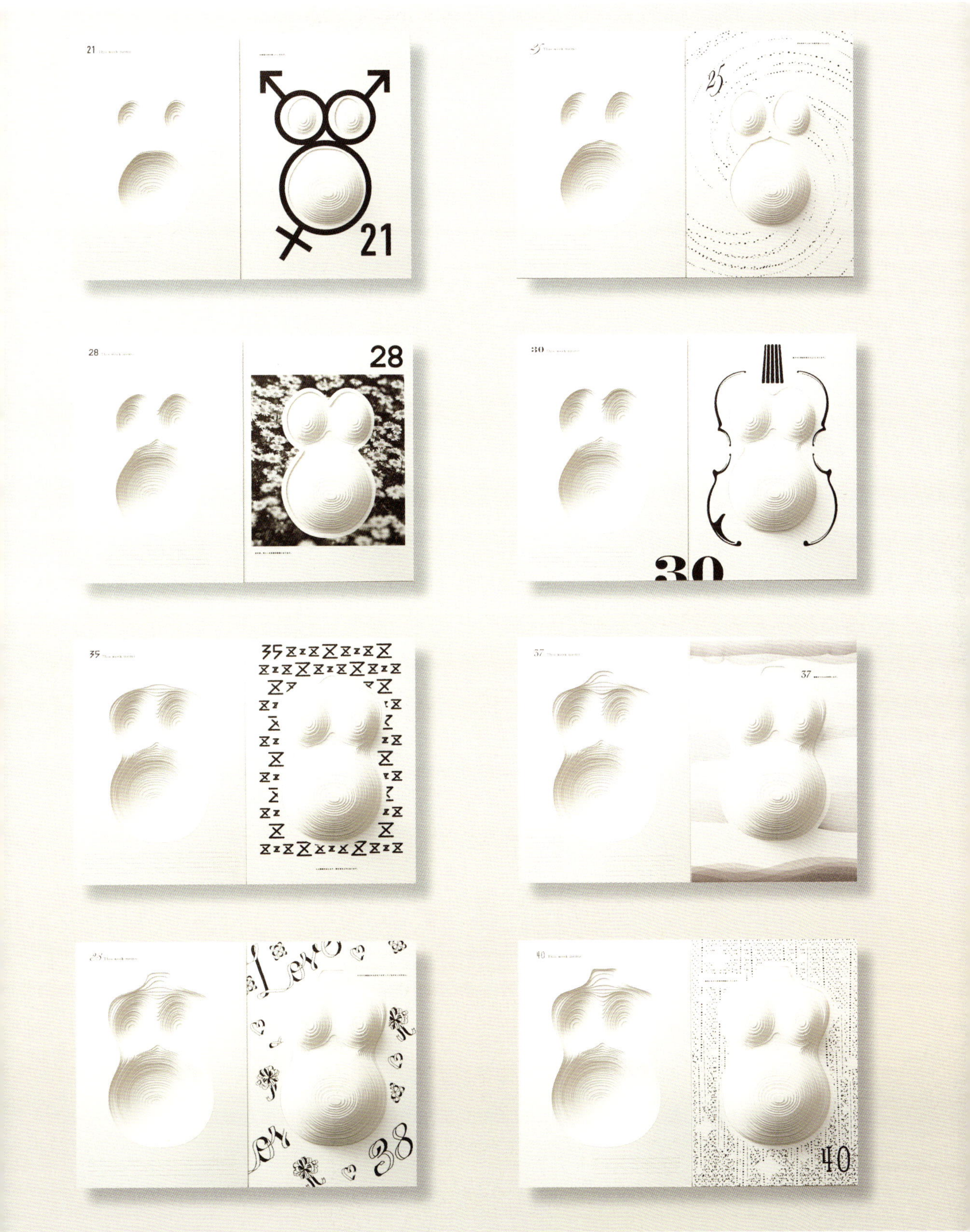
21
25
28
30
35
37
Love
38
40

Drawing the Writing

—Edited

The content of this book features a list of underrated artists throughout history, personally selected by the painter author. Providing a personal and authentic touch to the readers, this book is not just about writing but also about drawing. It is not just about writing but also drawing. To acknowledge the author's presense, marked by her feminity, layers of UV spot was applied to render the texture of a creased handkerchief on the cover. The deckle edge gives the book a raw and rugged feel.

Effects Spot colour, UV varnishing

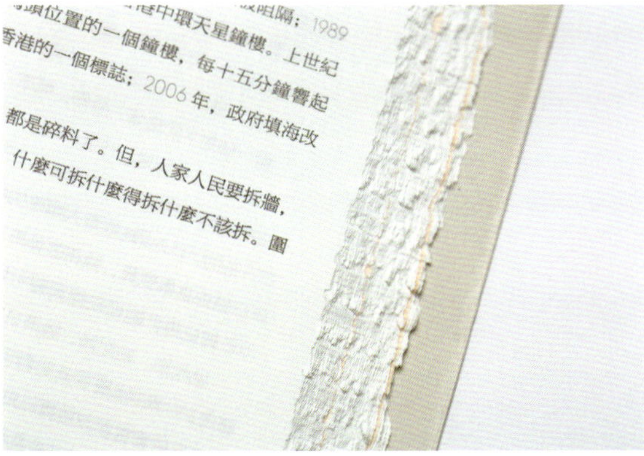

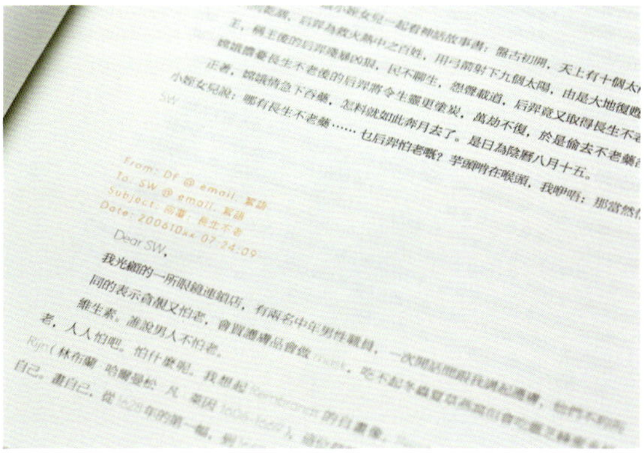

Dangerous Liaisons

—Éva Valicsek

When redesigning the iconic novel "Dangerous Liaisons" by Pierre Choderlos de Laclos, Éva Valicsek decided to show the duality of the story about the amoral schemes of two men, composed entirely as a conversation over letters. One point of view can be read horizontally on one side of the spread, and the response is printed vertically on the other. The idea of contrast extends further to the edge of book, with both "YES" or "NO" printed on both sides of the page margin. Either words pop out as the reader bends the book.

Typography Dolly & Auto
Photo Nóra Dénes
Video Balázs Balogh
Effects Die cutting, technical folding, special binding, fore-edge printing

NU

NO

to see you today, my love,
I beg you to accept with indulgence
Instead of coming straight
of the Comtesse de —, whose
and invited myself to dinner.
to Paris, and I went to the Opera,
When the opera was over I went
green room: there I found my old friend
by numerous admirers, as many
she was giving supper that evening
joined the company than, by
with them. I was also issued

For Browsing Only

—A Beautiful Design

The Browsing Copy was created as a non-commercial project to revive unloved books. A Beautiful Design gathered these forgotten books and invited a group of designers for each series from around the world to contribute and give them a second life. The original books and end results were documented and compiled into a catalogue to be exhibited in bookstores around the world. A limited run of only 300 copies were produced and customised with hand-torn covers in layers.

Client The Browsing Copy Project
Photo John Nursalim
Web design partner Jonathan Yuen
Effects Tearing

92/300

The Drinkable Book

—Brian Gartside (DDB New York)

Designers, scientists at the university of Virginia, and WATERisLIFE have come together to create a book to solve the problem of water-born diseases. Both an educational tool and a life saving resource, each page contains messages that educate safe water habits, and is coated with silver nanoparticles, a technologically advanced filtered paper that can purify contaminated water. The ink used for the filter is a food-grade ink specially created for this project, and the plastic book case can act as a filter machine.

Client WATERisLIFE
Design & production DDB New York (Matt Eastwood, Menno Kluin, Sam Shepherd, Frank Cartagena, Juan Carlos Pagan, Brian Gartside, Aaron Stephenson)
Printer Jamie Mahoney
Chemist Dr Theresa Dankovich
Effects Special ink, letterpress, laser cutting

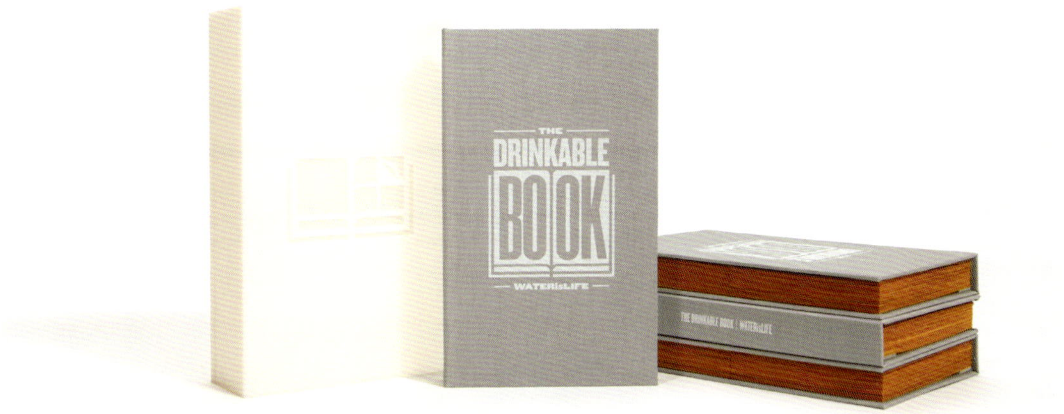
THE
DRINKABLE
BOOK
WATERisLIFE
THE DRINKABLE BOOK | WATERisLIFE

THE WATER IN YOUR VILLAGE
MAY CONTAIN DEADLY DISEASES.
EACH PAGE OF THIS BOOK IS
A PAPER WATER FILTER THAT
WILL MAKE IT SAFE TO DRINK.

THE
DRINKABLE
BOOK
WATERisLIFE
THE DRINKABLE BOOK | WATERisLIFE

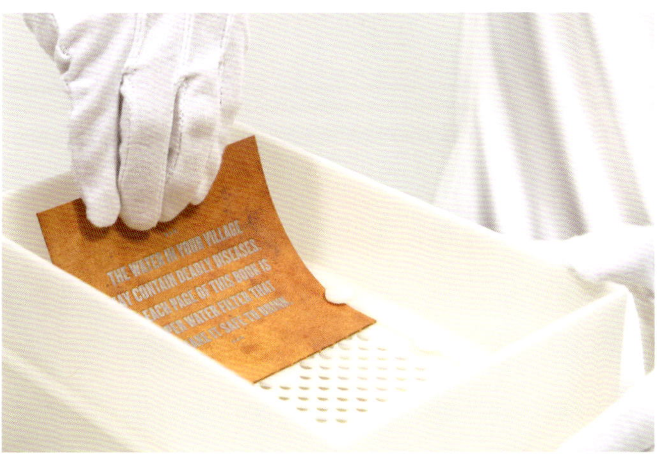
THE WATER IN YOUR VILLAGE
EACH PAGE OF THIS BOOK IS

DRINKABLE
BOOK

Transversal

—Buenos días,

Transversal is a biennial competition hosted by the Foundation for the International Biennial of Contemporary Art of Seville (BIACS) where designers in Seville can showcase their plans for the city. The book collates the finalists' entries targetting five locations along the East-West axis of Seville, and on the cover, five die cut rectangles twisting into a hollow space to underline the theme, hinting at the trail and the "intervention" of space. The various papers were hand-stitched together to compile the book.

Client Seville University
Effects Die cutting, hot stamping, technical binding

TRANSVERSAL
TRANSVERSAL
Transversal
TRANSVERSAL

Poetics of Harmony

—Soh Jin Ping

In this set of three books, embossing, handstitching and hand cut techniques are used to explaining different principals of Taoism through design. The first uses prints to show the dynamics of Yin and Yang, the second applies the grid of a Loshu diagram to trace the patterns of the five elements, and the last book uses a series of paper cuts to represent the message of harmony of triple unity between heaven, earth and mankind.

Photo Wong Jing Wei
Effects Handcutting, embossing & debossing, technical binding

萬物化生

Future from the Crossroads

—ACST Design

Documenting the research, design proposals and experimental projects of the Urban Regeneration station project in Taiwan, this book captures new ideas and the possibility for change in an urban setting. Taking the idea of "Crossroads", a street map of the project location, Zhongshan District, was embossed on its cover with both its English and Chinese titles placed in perpendicular to visualise the concept.

Client JUT Foundation For Arts & Architecture
Effects Embossing & debossing, screenprinting

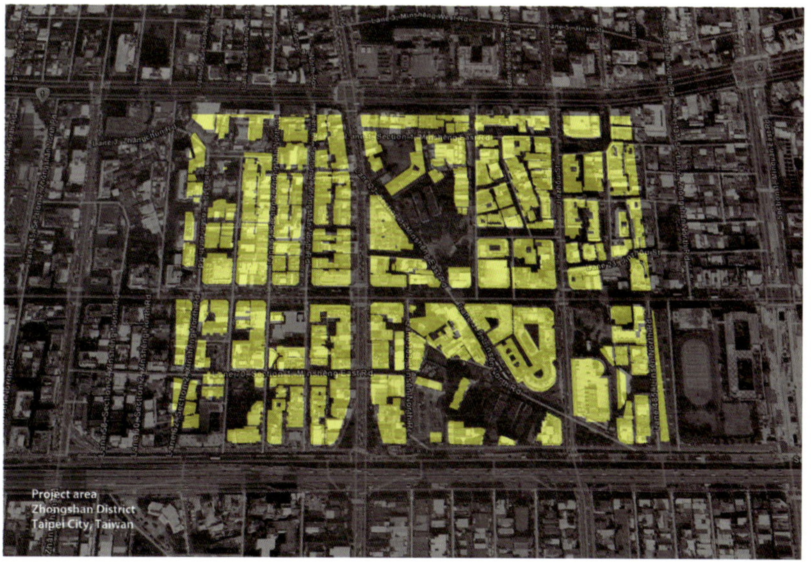
Project area
Zhongshan District
Taipei City, Taiwan

Recollection

—ACST Design

Recollection is a special book marking the achievements of Taiwan e-Learning and Digital Archives Programme. The tree growth ring embossed on its cover not only symbolises time and accomplishments but also responds to the title that every project in the book contributes to the programme's past, present and future. Likened to the programme's diversity, the jacket poster highlights the major feats on tracing paper that changes colour when placed upon different backgrounds.

Client Institute of History and Philology of Academia Sinica, Taiwan
Effects Technical folding, hot stamping, embossing, screenprinting

Re-
tion
記
憶

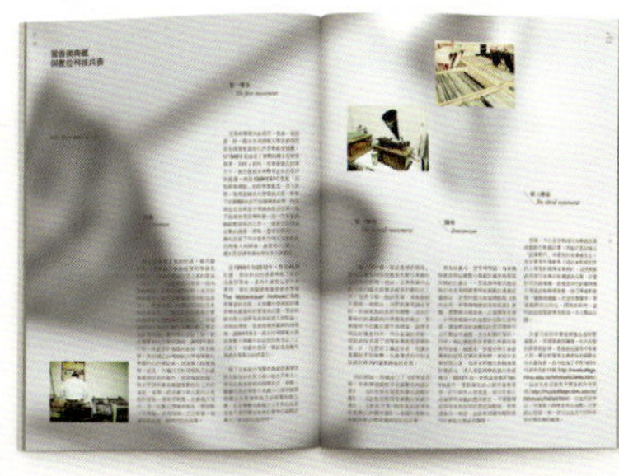

Re-
collec-
tion
記
憶
Achievements of
the Taiwan e-Learning and
Digital Archives Program
2011.11
The World Digital Library Includes 31
Ancient Books from the National Central
Library Collection
2010.12.10
A Retrospective is Held
of Its Achievements

Typeforce 3 Exhibition Catalog

—Firebelly Design

Serving as both a review of Typeforce gallery and celebrating each artist featured in the show, this book design honours typographic tradition, simple mark making and hand-carved stone forms. The idea was complemented with strips of light peeking through. Each book has a double cover sealed and affixed by hand.

Client Public Media Institue
Production Graphic Arts Studio, Delta Press Inc.
Paper Unisource Worldwide, Domtar
Effects Die cutting, spot colour, hot stamping, embossing, technical binding

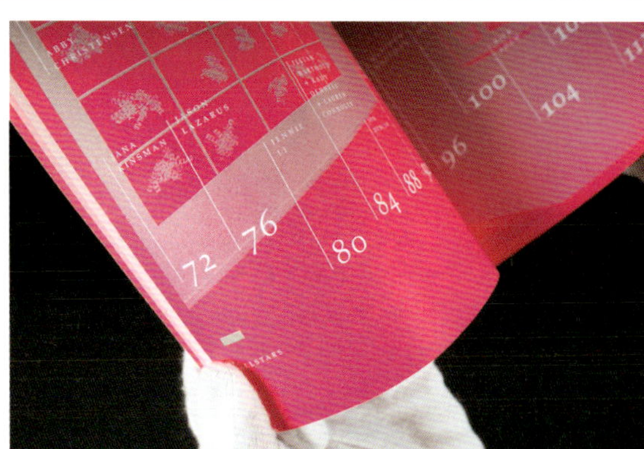

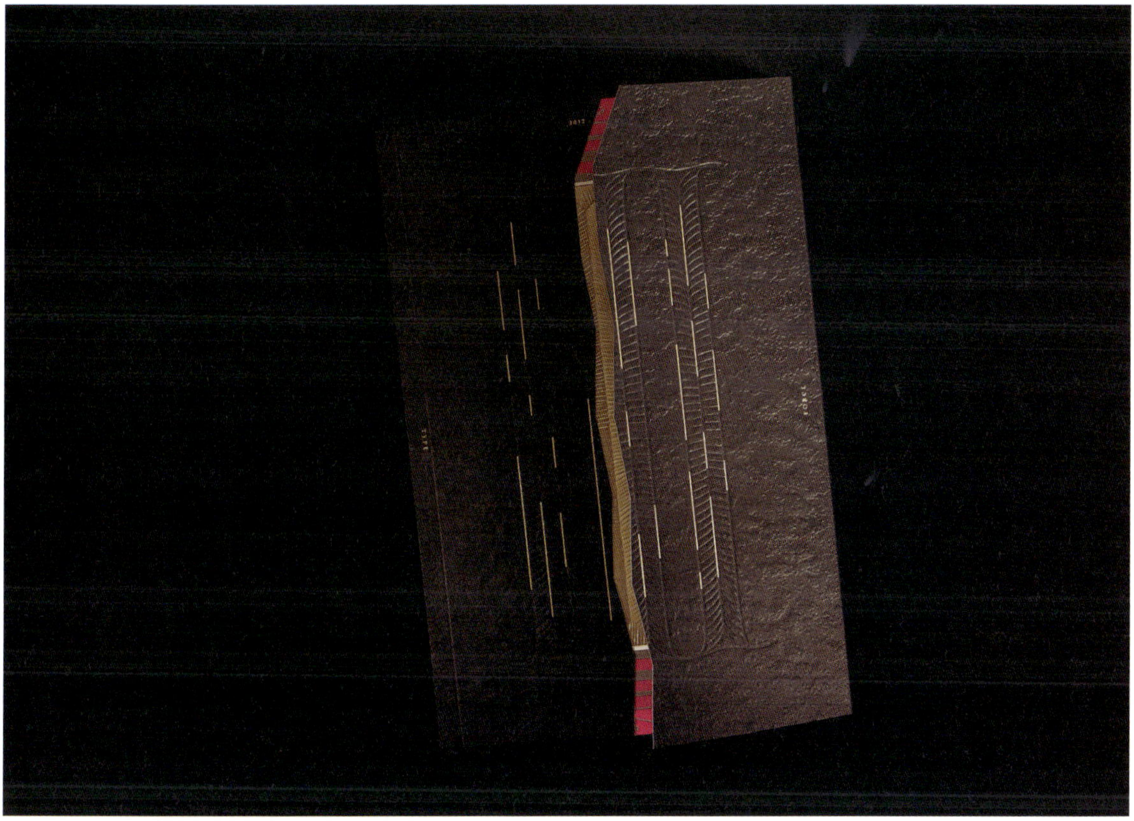

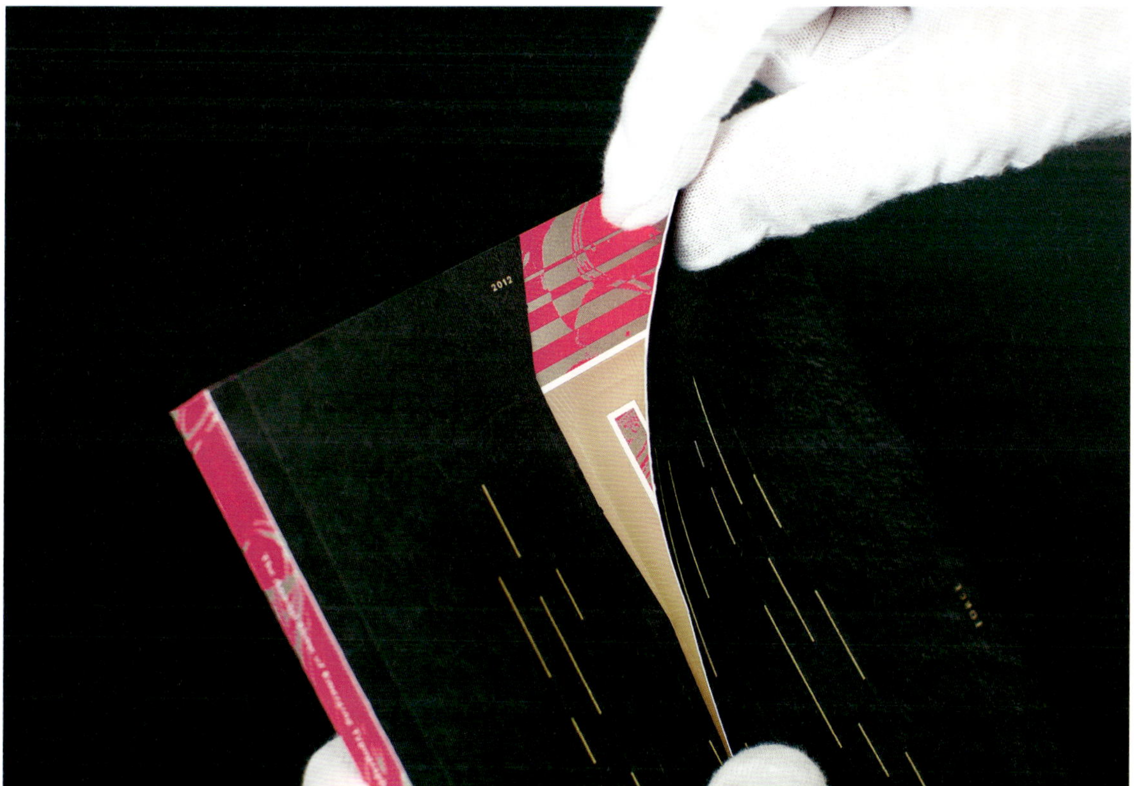

OPENED
MARCH 30

TYPE
FORCE

2012

Typographia

—Studio Much

This paper promotion for Polytrade takes its name from "typography". Offset printing, playing with shapes and typography are employed to create a unique promotional folder. Within this collection, five different weights of sample paper are provided, featuring types that can be found of the street, put together with hand drawn letterings.

Client Polytrade
Photo Times Pang
Effects Die cutting, technical folding, spot colour, hot stamping, embossing

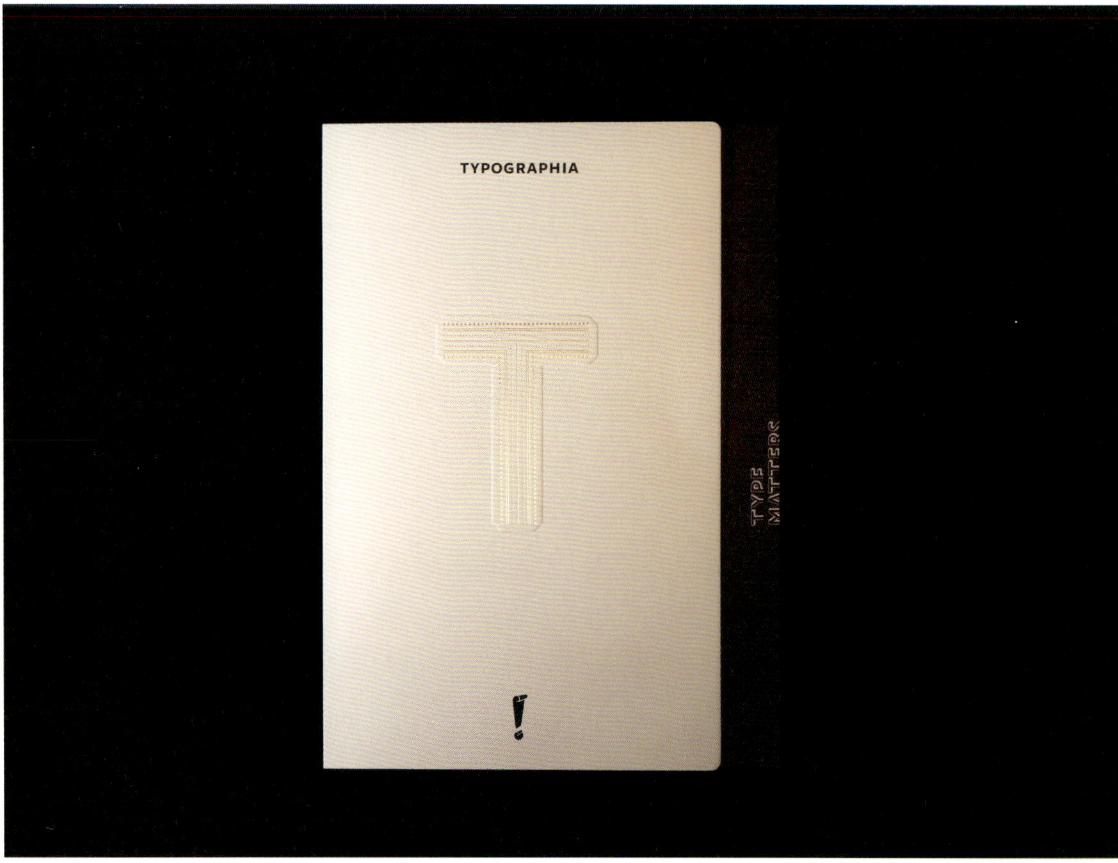

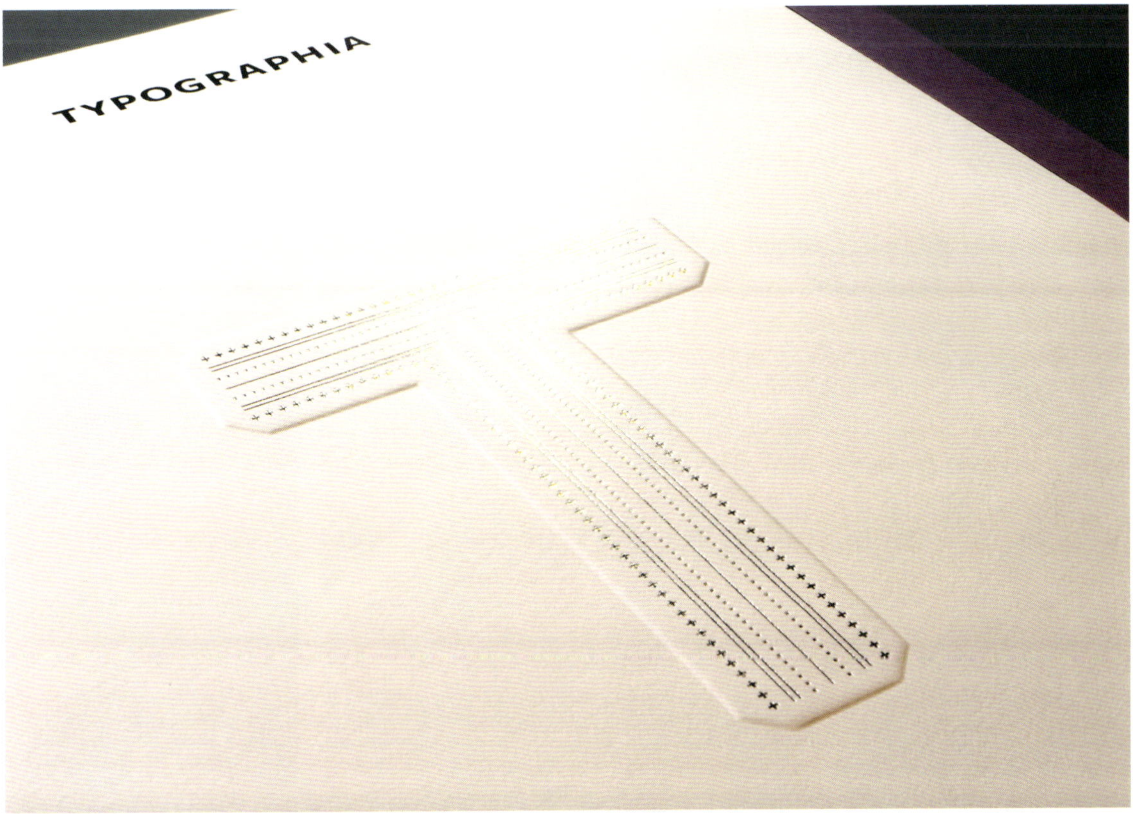
TYPOGRAPHIA

TYPOGRA
TYPE
MATTERS

NOTEBOOK #2 JAPAN

—OUWN

Recognised for their marvel with print techniques, OUWN was invited along with seven creative studios to each design a notebook for Imprimerie du Marais' second notebook project. The classic Grimoire-styled book of magic enchants with interactive technology, which allows printed numerals to dance on the users' phone screen as they scan the QR code on the opposite page. The QR codes and the two kings with micro-embossed details on the cover represent OUWN's and the Japanese tale of a yin-yang enchanter.

Client Imprimerie du Marais
Effects Hot stamping, embossing & micro-embossing, technical binding

NUMBERS
OUT OF PAPER,
START MOVING
WITH A WILL OF
THEIR OWN.

ENJOY THEIR DANCE
THE RIGHT ONE
CREATES THE NUMBERS,
AND THE LEFT ONE
BRINGS THEM TO LIFE.
THE ANIMATED
NUMBERS
SLIP OUT OF PAPER,
THEN START MOVING
WITH A WILL OF
THEIR OWN.
ENJOY THEIR DANCE LIKE
YOU WOULD
CARD GAMES.
THERE IS A
PAIR OF
WIZARDS HERE.

Do Not Just Hope & Dream

—Power-nap Over

Just about the size of a piece of A5 paper, this 64-page sketchbook aims to inspire dreamers to become believers. Taking on the setting of application forms, the covers urge users to be resolute in acting on their dreams, and start by penciling what's in their minds. Impressed blank fields encourage users to fortify commitments with names, a maxim and a time frame.

Effects Spot colour, debossing

PNO
VITA

PNO
VITA

DO NOT JUST DREAM
DO NOT JUST HOPE
DO NOT JUST DREAM

Fedrigoni Ispira Visual Book

—Happycentro

Designed to show Fedrigoni's Ispira collection at a glance, this paper catalogue resembles a stack of folders when closed and a burst of colour and texture when opened. Each paper of the visual book is narrated through changing amalgams of weights, sizes, inks, printing techniques and colours that are developed from the collection's palette. Either matching or contrasting, careful consideration has been put into arranging opposite pages.

Client Fedrigoni
Print management Studio Fasoli
Special credits Riccardo Zambelli
Effects Die cutting, spot colour, UV varnishing, hot stamping, embossing, technical binding

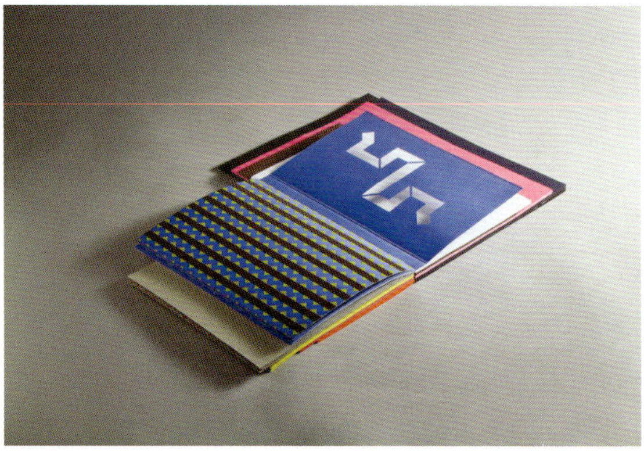

ISPIRA

Ispira.

Misomber Nuan Lookbook IV

—Somewhere Else

For Misomber Nuan's 2012 lookbook, the cover was designed to resemble the heat-treated leather material featured in the collection. Black acrylic paint was smeared across the cover on matte paper and black hot-stamped graphics, allowing the different finishings to stand out. The core idea behind the project was ideas of emptiness and voids, the promise of happenings, emotions and a dream to touch others through their experimental creations that guide Misomber Nuan's designs.

Client Misomber Nuan
Effects Hot stamping, non-paper materials, edge dipping

INCENDIE

—Alexia Roux

To help raise the awareness of the forest fires that devastated Cassis in 2010, Alexia Roux designed a unique book to view the aftermath in a realistic and evocative way. Starting with an illustration of thick black smoke on the cover, the book reveals burnt holes inside, carved out using a milling machine. Ingredients are directly applied onto the paper to enhance the graphic appearance and deliver an unpleasant odor of burnt matter to draw readers' attention to the seriousness of the incident.

Effects Perforation, screenprinting

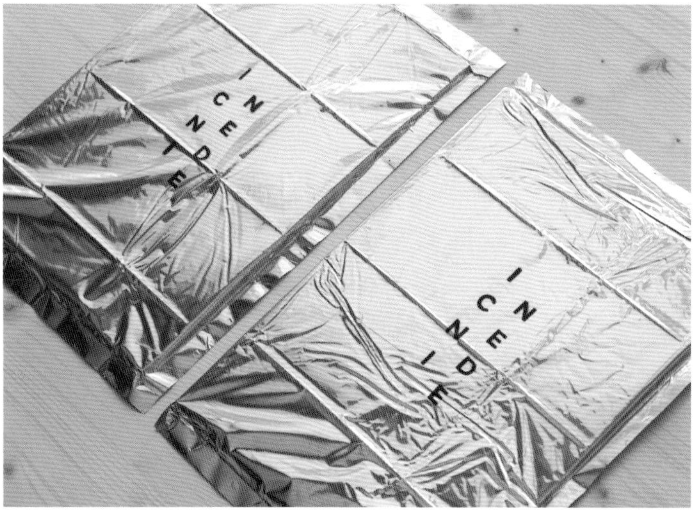

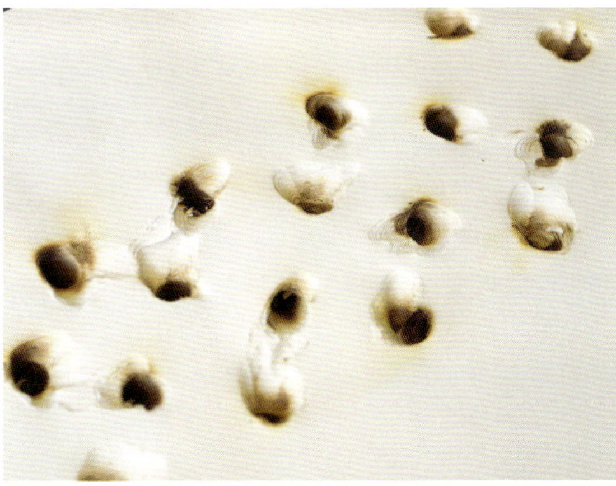

INCENDIE

In Good Hands

—Bruketa&Zinic OM

Delivering a message that the company is in good hands of its employees who are also the owners, Adris Group's annual report, "In Good Hands", was printed with thermal colour. On the outside, as the palm of the hands touches the book, a green background and floral details reveals itself. The same ink was also used to produce the illustrations inside. A digital iPad version was also developed with the same interactive effect.

Client Adris Group
Creative team Davor Bruketa, Nikola Zinic, Nebojsa Cvetkovic, Neven Crljenak, Vesna Durasin, Radovan Radicevic
Illustration Vedran Klemens
Photo Domagoj Kunic
Effects Special ink, hot stamping, laser cutting

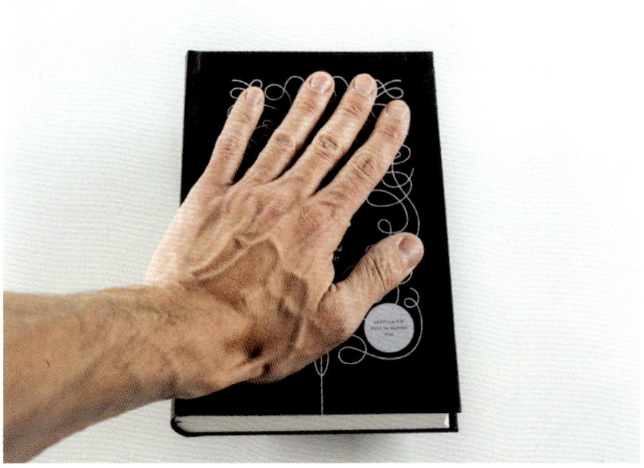

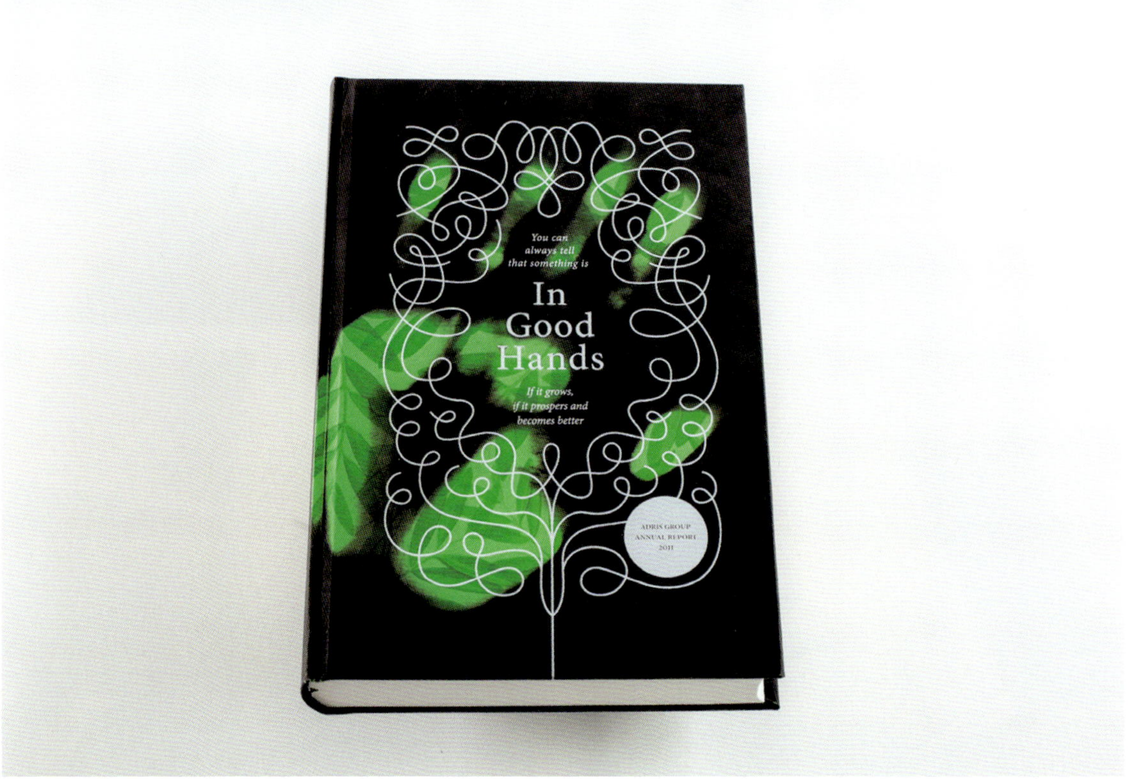

Hands can achieve anything.
7.6

Hands can achieve anything.
7.6

In Good Hands

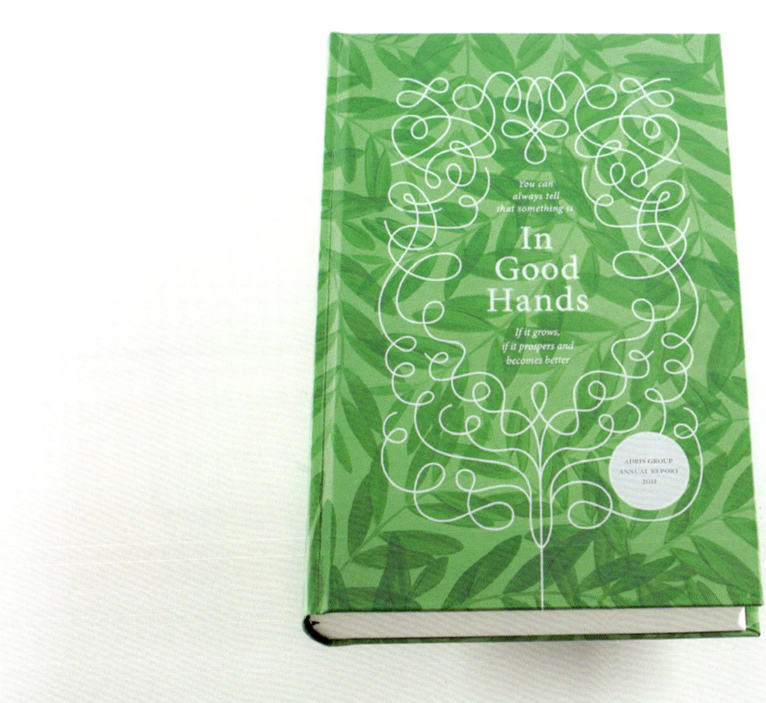
You can always tell that something is
In Good Hands
If it grows, if it prospers and becomes better
ADRIS GROUP ANNUAL REPORT 2011

7 Days In Myanmar

—Asylum

7 Days in Myanmar portrays Myanmar through 30 international photographers' lens over a seven-day period. The numerous locations these photographers trod were foil-blocked onto an invisible map of the country on the photo book's textured hardcover. Symbolic of Burmese faith, a Buddhist motif was adopted for the slipcase. While the public edition used participant Frenchman Bruno Barbey's picture, the deluxe limited edition took on distressed gold foil stamping inspired by gilded statues, which was gifted to ministers and important delegates.

Client Editions Didier Millet
Effects Hot stamping

7 DAYS
IN MYANMAR
30
PHOTOGRAPHERS
7 DAYS
IN MYANMAR
30
PHOTOGRAPHERS

7 DAYS
IN MYANMAR
30 PHOTOGRAPHERS
ABBAS / AUNG PYAE / BRUNO BARBEY / BARRY BROMAN /
CHANG CHIEN-CHI / ALAIN COMPOST / MICHAEL FREEMAN / MATT GRACE /
RIO HELMI / CATHERINE KARNOW / KAUNG HTET / KYAW KYAW WINN /
LYNN BO BO / STEVE MCCURRY / MINZAYAR / ATHIT PERAWONGMETHA /
RAGHU RAI / GILLES SABRIÉ / SAI KHAM LYNN / DOMINIC SANSONI /
SC SHEKAR / SOE ZEYA TUN / TARA SOSROWARDOYO /
CHRIS STEELE-PERKINS / NAT SUMANATEMEYA / MELISA TEO /
THET HTOO / JOHN VINK / MICHAEL YAMASHITA / YE AUNG THU
Foreword by
Dr Thant Myint-U
Text by
John Falconer
Denis Gray
Dr Thaw Kaung
Patrick Winn
Nicholas Grossman
edm

Graphic Digits

—viction workshop ltd

Graphic Digits is a book exploring examples and the application of modern numeral design. The jacket design pays homage to transfer lettering, a popular and economic way to apply high quality typography prior to the digital age. Foil-stamped on a tracing paper and enhanced in a shiny gold, letters and numbers spell out the book's title in a style faithful to the lettering sheets, accompanied with each types' specification.

Client victionary
Effects Hot stamping

GRAPHIC DIGITS
New typographic approach to numerals
G/05
GD1421
60pt 31mm
GD1422
38pt 20mm

Hanzi · Kanji · Hanja

—viction workshop ltd

Hanzi · Kanji · Hanja examines contemporary Chinese character designs in present graphic languages. Taking Taiwanese professor Lee Ken-tsai's work for Type Directors Club as the base, the book's jacket heightens the beautiful components of Chinese characters with bold neon inks against black. Where the book's Chinese and English title overlaps and quadruples on the cover, special effects such as laser-cut lines, silver ink and UV varnishing give the multiple information a distinctive layering.

Client victionary
Special credits Lee Ken-tsai
Effects Spot colour, UV varnishing, laser cutting, edge dipping

HANZI
KANJI
HANJA
Graphic & Logo Design with
Contemporary Chinese Characters

HANZI · KANJI · HANJA
Graphic & logo design with contemporary chinese characters
Graphic & Logo Design with
Contemporary Chinese Characters

Welcome to Taiwan's Old Theatre

— Kuan-li Tang, Cavis Huang, Jhih-ting Chen

Taiwan's historical theatres are disappearing. However, nine of these iconic theatres and their 20th-century decor can be found in their complete form in these pop up books, posters and time-lapse documentary films, both celebrating their grandeur and raising awareness of their plight. Each architecture comes in a small black box. The matte cover is the first point of interaction, which reveals a full 3D model, street views, a district map and captions giving details of respective theatres' background and current state.

Effects Technical folding, hot stamping, laser cutting, non-paper materials, technical binding

築夢黑箱
Welcome to Taiwan`s Old Theater

院戲臺舞大

院 戲 灣 內

新竹

築夢黑箱

One Point Six One Eight

—StudioKALEIDO

This deceptively simple cover, spattered with loose paper fibres, defines perfection in contrast to its mathematically calculated layout design. Responding to the content of migration and perfection, the book unfolds an accordion, with one definite black spiral, to reflect the loop of immigration patterns in a 'no beginning and end' fashion. A full-black graphic is printed on grey chipboard, producing a raw, speckled effect on the cover.

Client Ethos Books
Effects Die cutting, technical folding

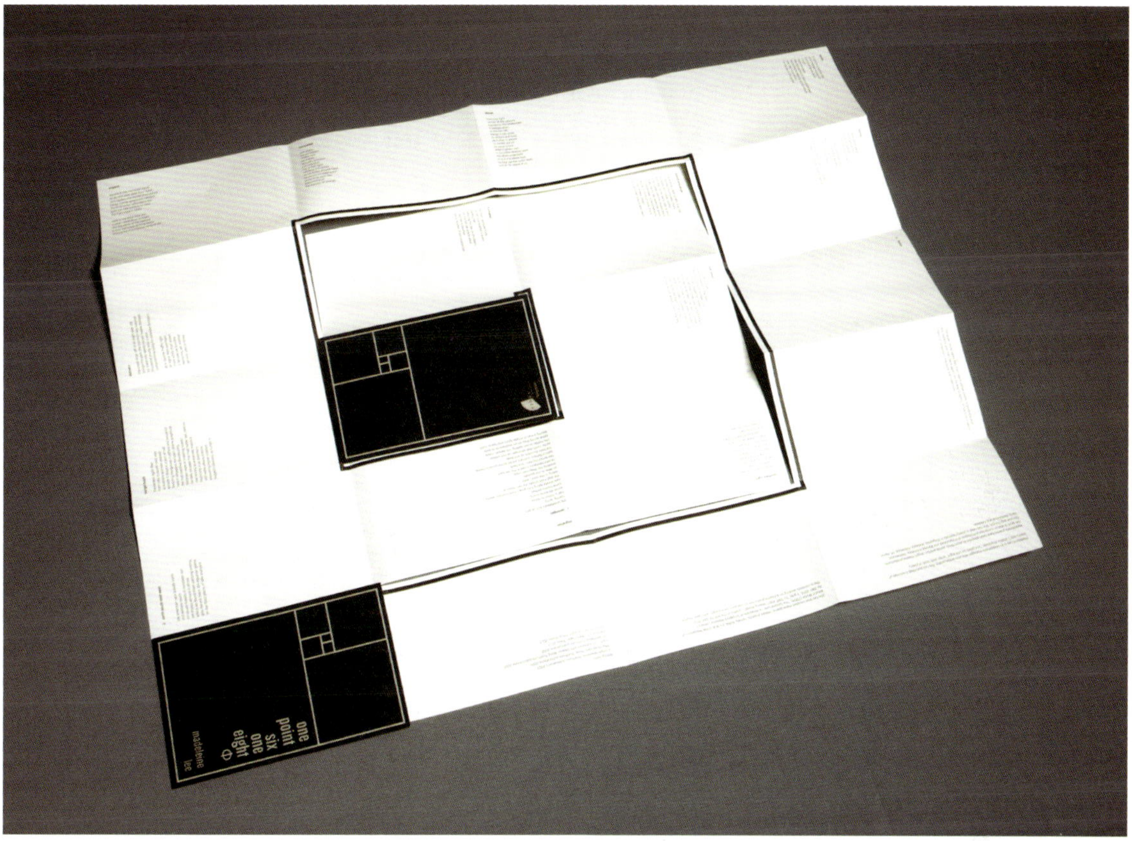
one
point
six
one
eight
Φ
madeleine
lee

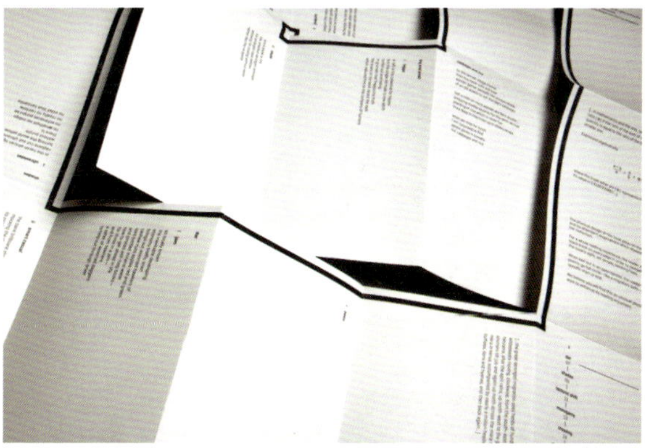

one
point
six
one
eight
Φ
madeleine
lee

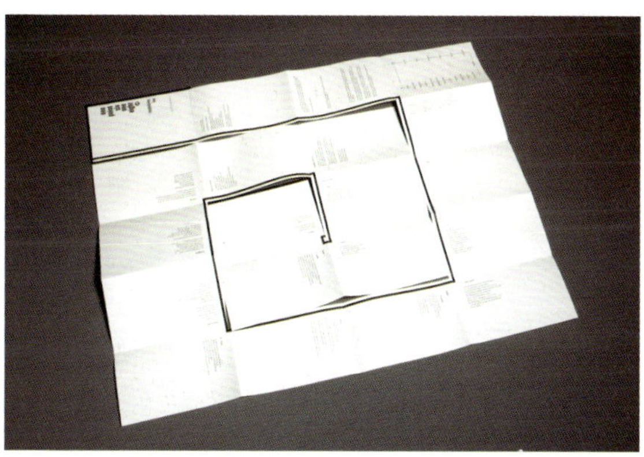

FOOD. CHOCOLATE. DESIGN.

—Happycentro

In collaboration with chocolate Sabadì as leitmotiv, Happycentro championed an event at Florence Pitti 2013 Taste Fair bringing together Italian food artisans, food bloggers and designers. As a result, 16 Italian graphic designers interpreted and translated 16 recipes into images. Memories of this experiment and the works exhibited were condensed into a precious volume, where vivid colours on the exposed spine and fun debossed logotype showoff local vibe.

Effects Die cutting, spot colours, embossing & debossing, technical binding, duplex

FOOD. CHOCOLATE. DESIGN.
1 CHOCOLATE MAKER
8 FOOD CRAFTSMEN
8 FOOD BLOGGERS
16 SPECIAL RECIPES
16 GRAPHIC DESIGNERS
1 COLLECTIVE PROJECT

CACIO E PEPE

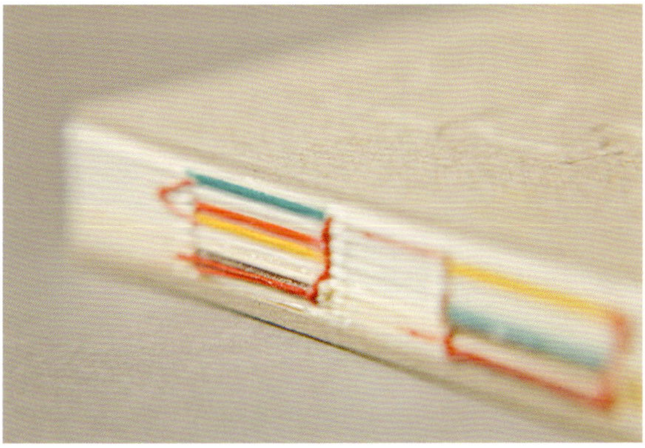

Posters & Invitations

Posters & Invitations
Posters & Invitations
Posters & Invitations
Posters & Invitations
Posters & Invitations
Posters & Invitations
Posters & Invitations
Posters & Invitations

Fabienne Levy, Norbert Bisky

— Balmer Hählen

Norbert Bisky, a German artist based in Berlin, is deemed one of the most important representatives of new figurative painting in the 21st century. For his exhibition in Fabienne Levy, a creative/gallery space in Lausanne, at the end of 2020, the team at Balmer Hählen designed eye-catching posters featuring beautiful techniques to promote his show.

Client Fabienne Levy
Printing Lézard Graphique
Effects Spot colour, UV varnishing, special ink, screenprinting

FABIENNE LEVY
27.11.20–
13.02.21
Norbert Bisky
Unrest
FABIENNE LEVY
AVENUE LOUIS-RUCHONNET 6
1003 LAUSANNE
WWW.FABIENNELEVY.COM
FABIENNE
LEVY
The true fight
against injustice
rests in our capacity to
accept differences
FABIENNE LEVY
AVENUE LOUIS-RUCHONNET 6
1003 LAUSANNE
WWW.FABIENNELEVY.COM

Independent Paper Show 2020

— Balmer Hählen

Dedicated to paper and printing techniques, the Independent Paper Show in Lausanne showcases qualitative works made in the graphic arts field. To reflect the nature of the show as well as the reputable producers, suppliers and paper shapers being featured, the team at Balmer Hählen designed a 'Save the Date' invitation for its 2020 edition, highlighting creative techniques and quality materials.

Client Independent Paper Show 2020
Printing Sonderegger AG
Effects Hot stamping, UV varnishing, embossing

Independent
Paper
Show
with
Lorenz Boegli
Bubu
Sonderegger
and
the best paper
producers
and suppliers
papershow
.ch
6+7
May
2020
Lausanne
Flon
Rue de Genève
19

with
Lorenz Boegli
Bubu
Sonderegger
and
the best paper
producers
and suppliers
papershow
.ch
Save
6+7
May
2020
Lausanne
Flon
Rue de Genève
19

5 Years Greeting Card

— Balmer Hählen

Balmer Hählen develops different types of mediums such as print, digital and textile materials through design exploration from the studio's base in Lausanne. In celebrating its five-year anniversary as well as its specialisation in paper and printing techniques, the team created a greeting card that was printed in Switzerland with holographic foil.

Printing Atelier Typo de la Cité
Effects Hot stamping, debossing, letterpress

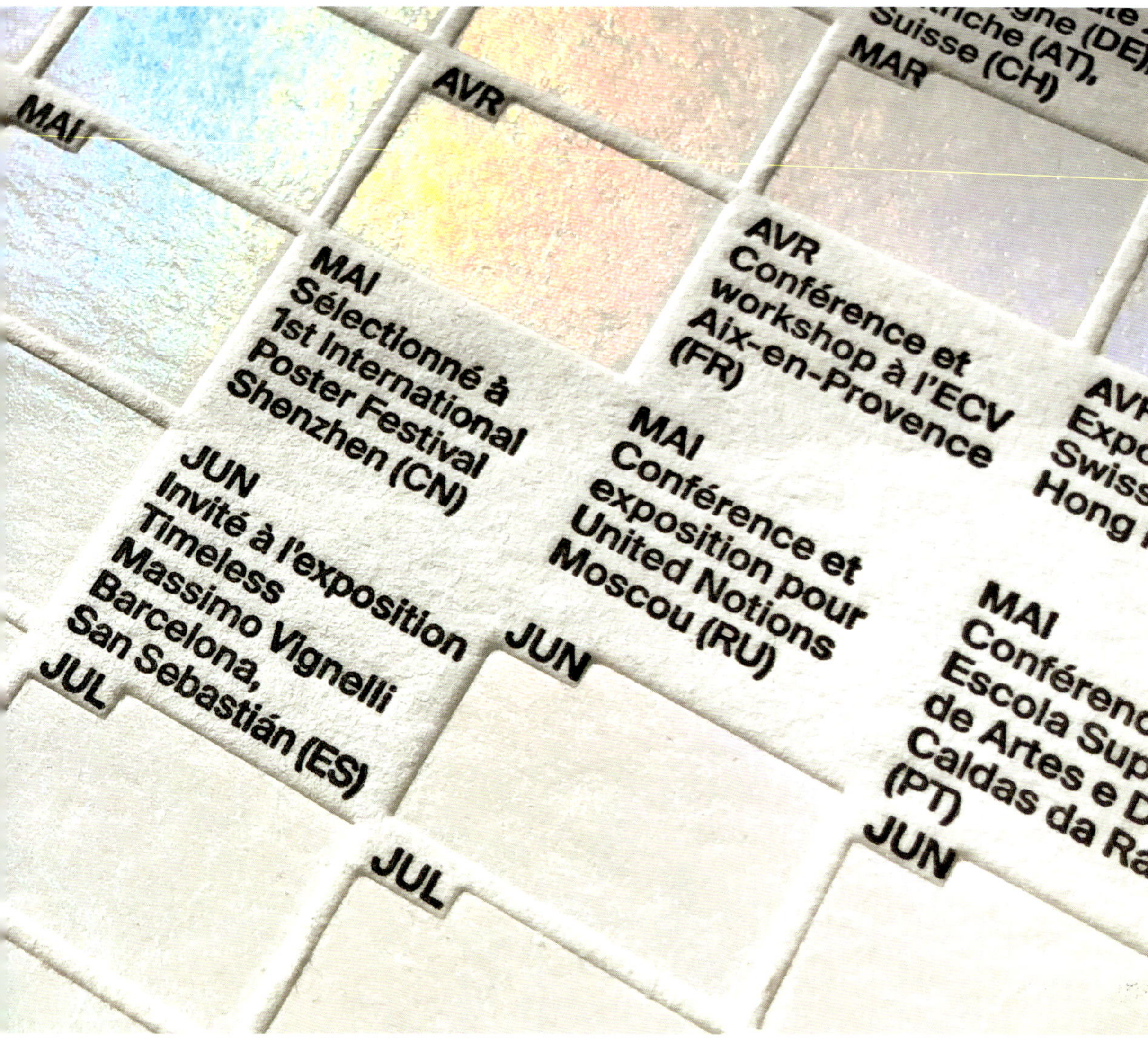

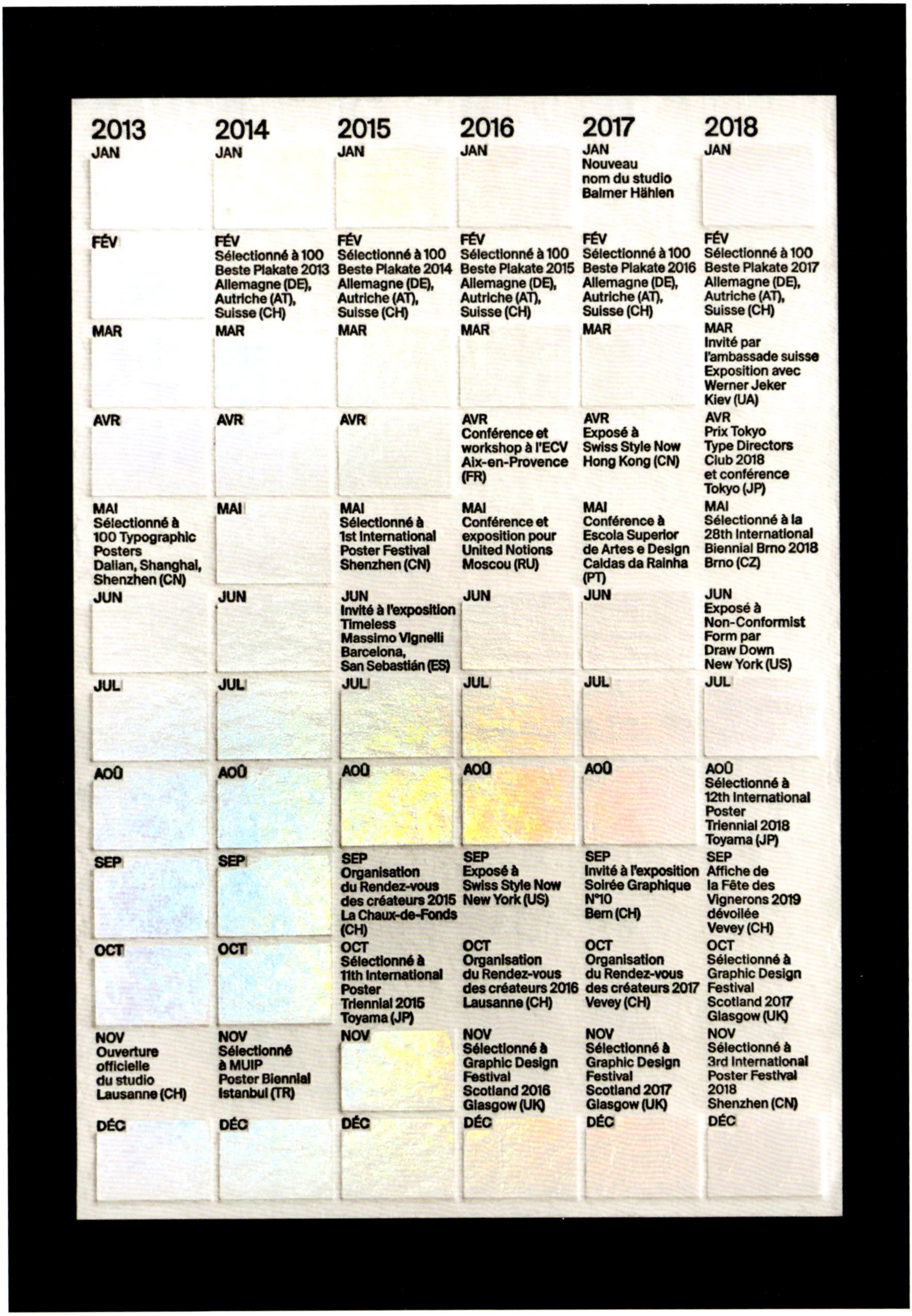
2013
JAN
FÉV
MAR
AVR
MAI Sélectionné à 100 Typographic Posters Dalian, Shanghai, Shenzhen (CN)
JUN
JUL
AOÛ
SEP
OCT
NOV Ouverture officielle du studio Lausanne (CH)
DÉC
2014
JAN
FÉV Sélectionné à 100 Beste Plakate 2013 Allemagne (DE), Autriche (AT), Suisse (CH)
MAR
AVR
MAI
JUN
JUL
AOÛ
SEP
OCT
NOV Sélectionné à MUIP Poster Biennial Istanbul (TR)
DÉC
2015
JAN
FÉV Sélectionné à 100 Beste Plakate 2014 Allemagne (DE), Autriche (AT), Suisse (CH)
MAR
AVR
MAI Sélectionné à 1st International Poster Festival Shenzhen (CN)
JUN Invité à l'exposition Timeless Massimo Vignelli Barcelona, San Sebastián (ES)
JUL
AOÛ
SEP Organisation du Rendez-vous des créateurs 2015 La Chaux-de-Fonds (CH)
OCT Sélectionné à 11th International Poster Triennial 2015 Toyama (JP)
NOV
DÉC
2016
JAN
FÉV Sélectionné à 100 Beste Plakate 2015 Allemagne (DE), Autriche (AT), Suisse (CH)
MAR
AVR Conférence et workshop à l'ECV Aix-en-Provence (FR)
MAI Conférence et exposition pour United Notions Moscou (RU)
JUN
JUL
AOÛ
SEP Exposé à Swiss Style Now New York (US)
OCT Organisation du Rendez-vous des créateurs 2016 Lausanne (CH)
NOV Sélectionné à Graphic Design Festival Scotland 2016 Glasgow (UK)
DÉC
2017
JAN Nouveau nom du studio Balmer Hählen
FÉV Sélectionné à 100 Beste Plakate 2016 Allemagne (DE), Autriche (AT), Suisse (CH)
MAR
AVR Exposé à Swiss Style Now Hong Kong (CN)
MAI Conférence à Escola Superior de Artes e Design Caldas da Rainha (PT)
JUN
JUL
AOÛ
SEP Invité à l'exposition Soirée Graphique N°10 Bern (CH)
OCT Organisation du Rendez-vous des créateurs 2017 Vevey (CH)
NOV Sélectionné à Graphic Design Festival Scotland 2017 Glasgow (UK)
DÉC
2018
JAN
FÉV Sélectionné à 100 Beste Plakate 2017 Allemagne (DE), Autriche (AT), Suisse (CH)
MAR Invité par l'ambassade suisse Exposition avec Werner Jeker Kiev (UA)
AVR Prix Tokyo Type Directors Club 2018 et conférence Tokyo (JP)
MAI Sélectionné à la 28th International Biennial Brno 2018 Brno (CZ)
JUN Exposé à Non-Conformist Form par Draw Down New York (US)
JUL
AOÛ Sélectionné à 12th International Poster Triennial 2018 Toyama (JP)
SEP Affiche de la Fête des Vignerons 2019 dévoilée Vevey (CH)
OCT Sélectionné à Graphic Design Festival Scotland 2017 Glasgow (UK)
NOV Sélectionné à 3rd International Poster Festival 2018 Shenzhen (CN)
DÉC

Le Quotidien des Tranchees

—Alexia Roux

Once a political subject and a sign of invasion in a war zone, smell was used to create a message for the centenary exhibition of the First World War, appealing to a sense that's difficult to escape. Printed with a water resistant white ink on white blotting paper, the content of the poster only became visible as the paper soaked up the black as it's dipped in the ink on the launch day. Whiffs of the solution was expected to emanate from the poster and linger in the room.

Effects Special ink

DE LA
PREMIÈRE
GUERRE
MONDIALE
14—18
4 - 26/08/2014
le quotidien
des tranchées

GUERRE
MONDIALE
14—18
le quotidien
des tranchées

14—18
le quotidien
des tranchées

le quotidien
des tranchées

CENTENAIRE
DE LA
PREMIÈRE
GUERRE
MONDIALE

Risk vs. Reward

—Büro North

Created for a poster exhibition organised by The Design Kids in Melbourne, Büro North created a typographic poster using the words "Risk vs. Reward" printed in invisible ultraviolet ink. The poster was exhibited at the end of an alleyway, with only the word 'RISK' remaining constantly visible. A motion detecting UV light was close by, and when it was triggered, a flamboyant 'vs Reward' is revealed.

Client The Design Kids
Effects Special ink, laser cutting, screenprinting

RISK
RISK
vs
Reward

We Die For Beauty

—Carlos Bermúdez, Mau Morgó

Designed as a self-promotional piece of work, "We Die For Beauty" is a limited edition poster with just 200 copies —190 were given as gifts to other creatives in the field and the remaining ten were sold to the general public. The poster is made out of golden silkscreening ink over 150g/m² B2 size black paper.

Photo Roc Canals
Printing Leicrom
Effects Spot colour, screenprinting

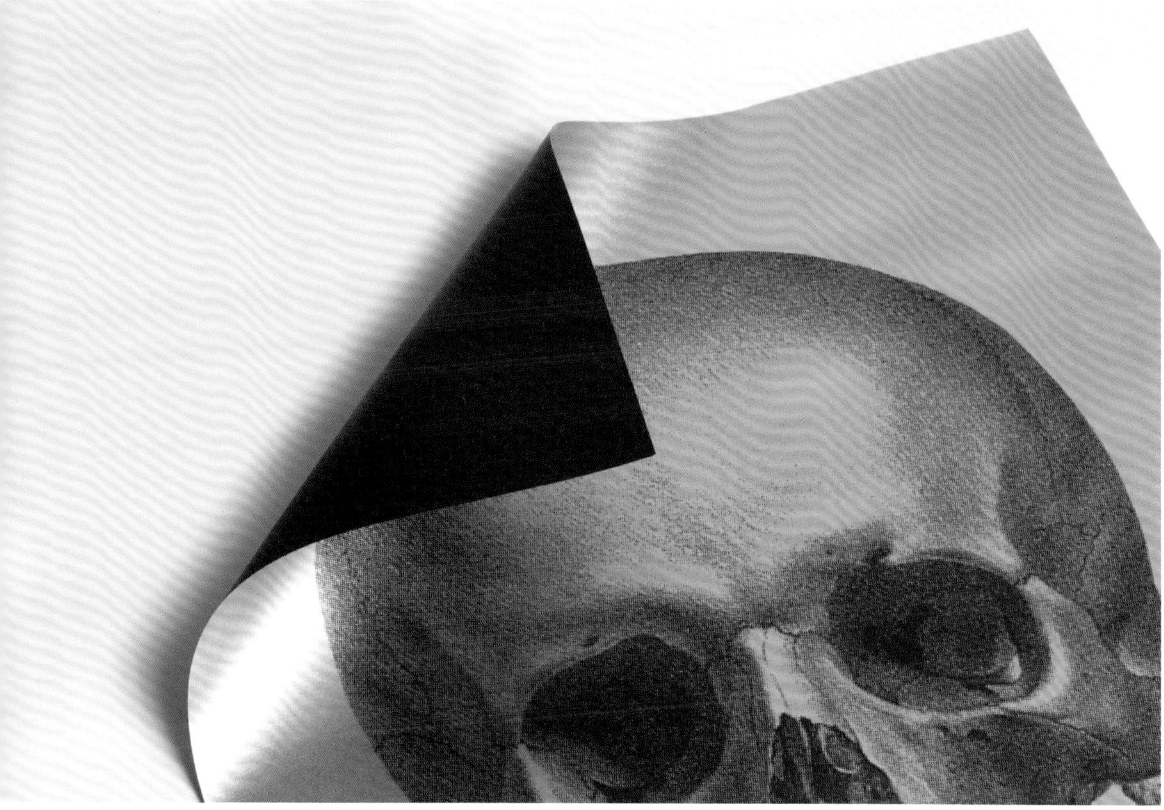

FEDRIGONI
ESPAÑA
Ispira Mistero 150gr/m2
www.fedrigoni.es
LEICROM
Printed with Pantone 871U
www.leicrom.com

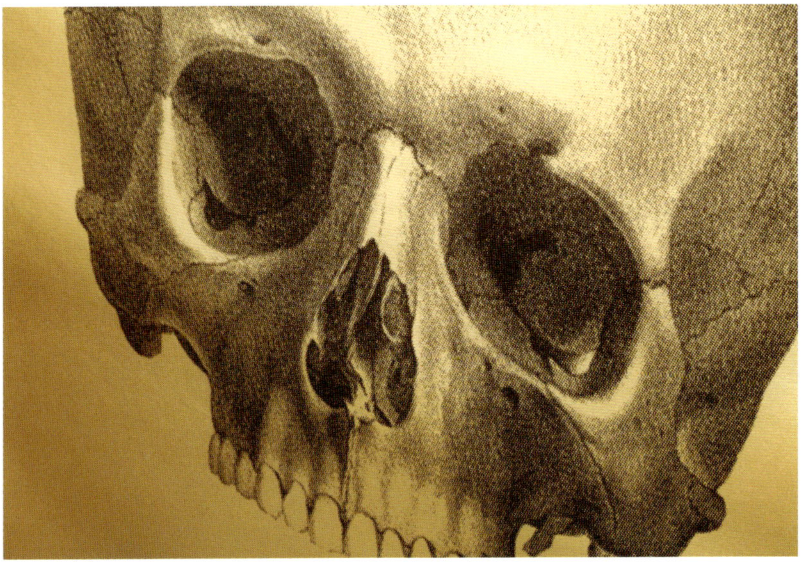

We die for beauty
145 of 200

Daily beautiful inspiration
o die for
www.wedieforbeauty.com
hello@wedieforbeauty.com

velilla

A3 Studio Invitation

—A3 Studio

The co-founders of A3 studio, Priscilla Balmer and Yvo Hählen, created this poster to announce their office relocation and the opening night. Printed on copper paper, the black lines in the design mimic a half open door, implying that visitors are most welcome. The embossing enhances the typography of the invitation by adding texture.

Photo Michel Meier
Effects Embossing, letterpress

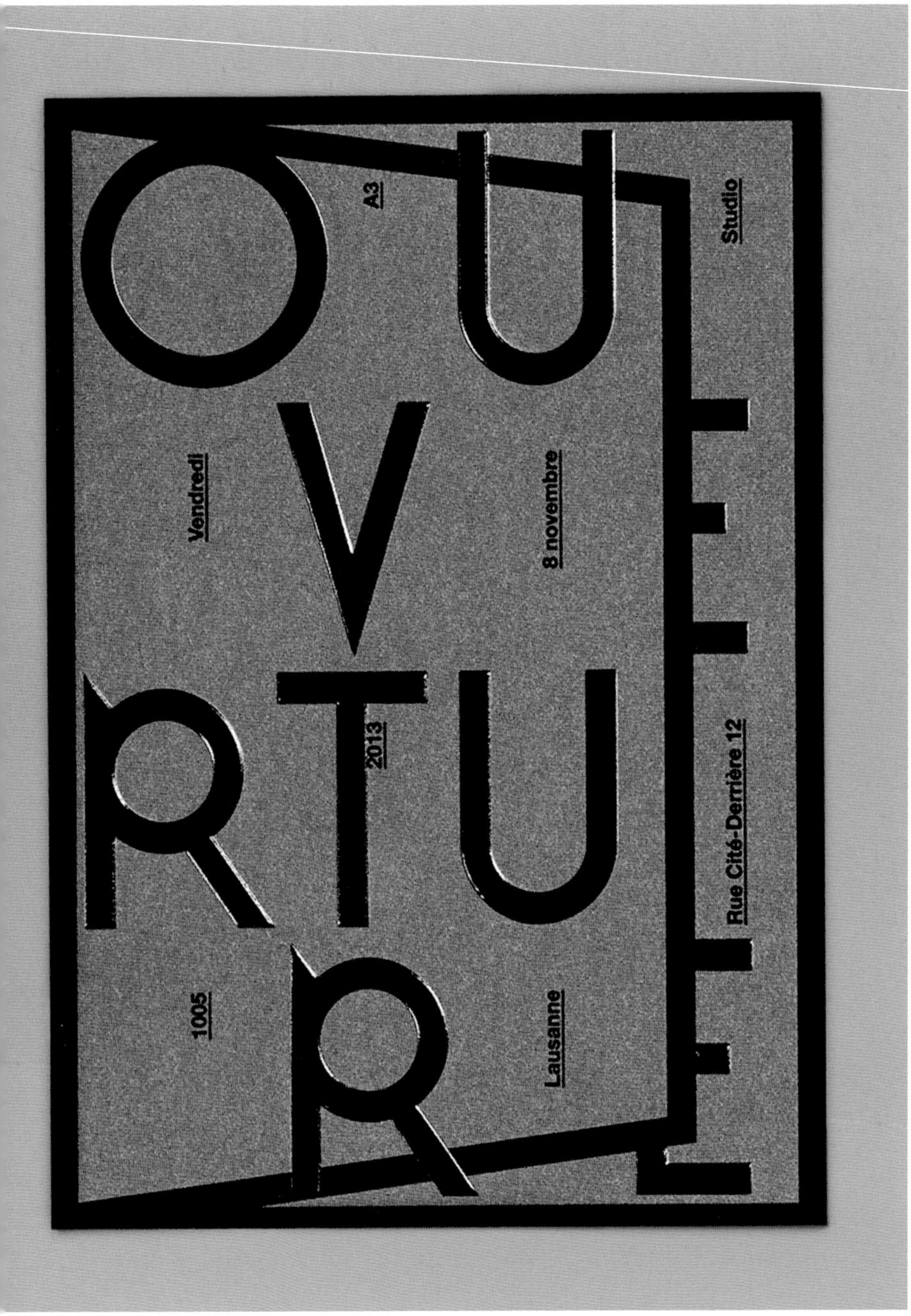

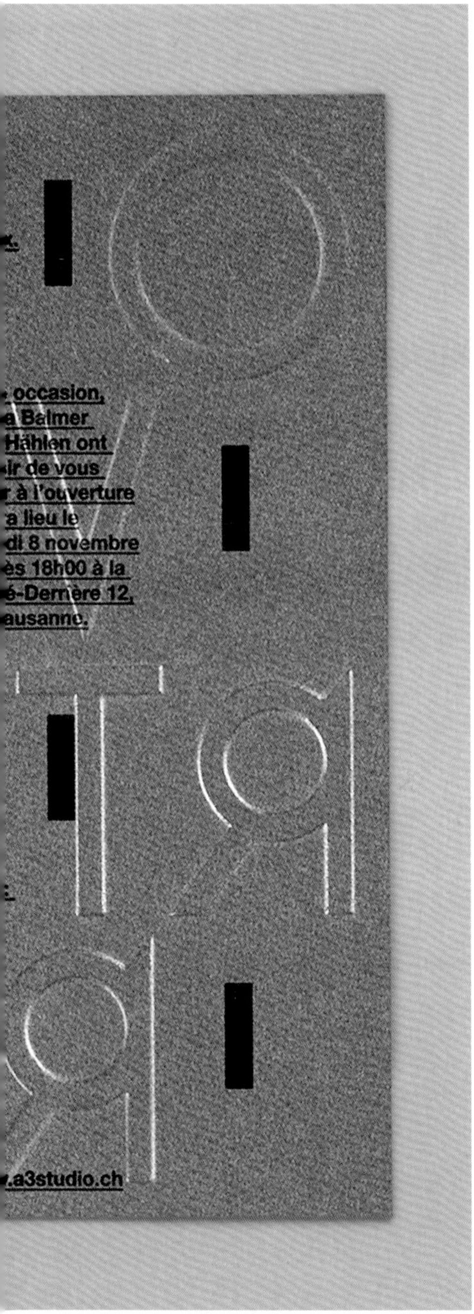
occasion,
a Balmer
Hählen ont
ir de vous
à l'ouverture
a lieu le
di 8 novembre
ès 18h00 à la
é-Derrière 12,
ausanne.
.a3studio.ch

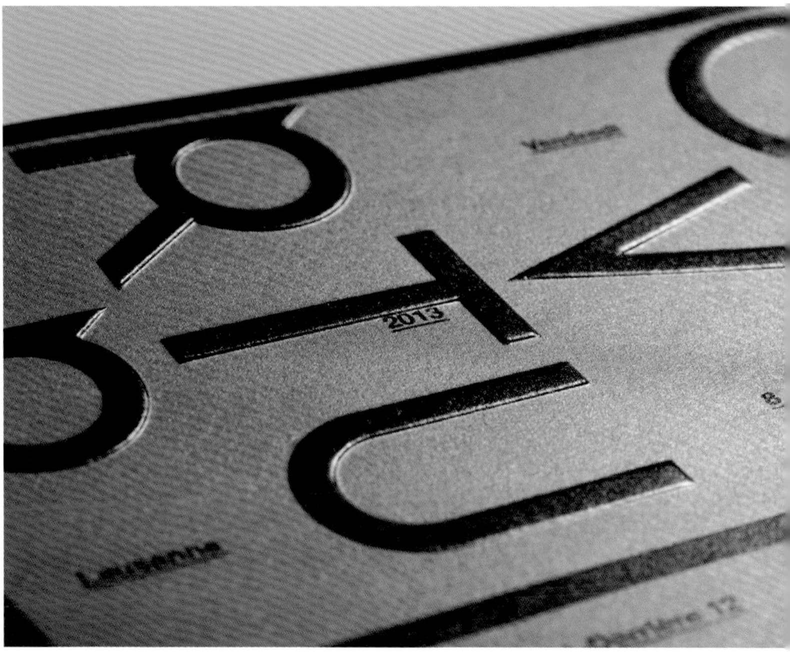
2013
Lausanne
Derrière 12

Handmade Structure

—NOSIGNER

Held in paper manufacturer Takeo's MIHONCHO HONTEN showroom, Handmade Structure was an exhibition that explored the appeal and capabilities of paper as a material. As a means of direct marketing, NOSIGNER created postcard and paper samples that resembles a wooden shingle construction. Made possible by rhombus trace lines, this handmade process is a taste of the many possibilities when paper meets structural design.

Client Takeo
Effects Technical folding, embossing

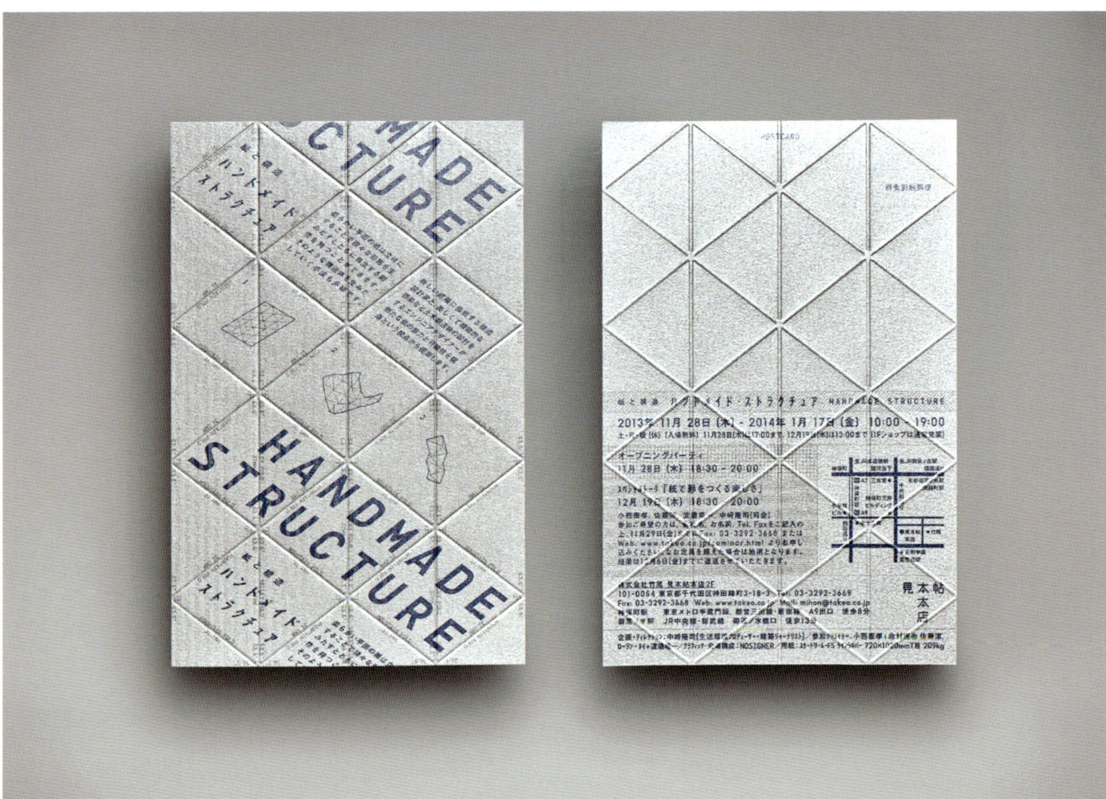

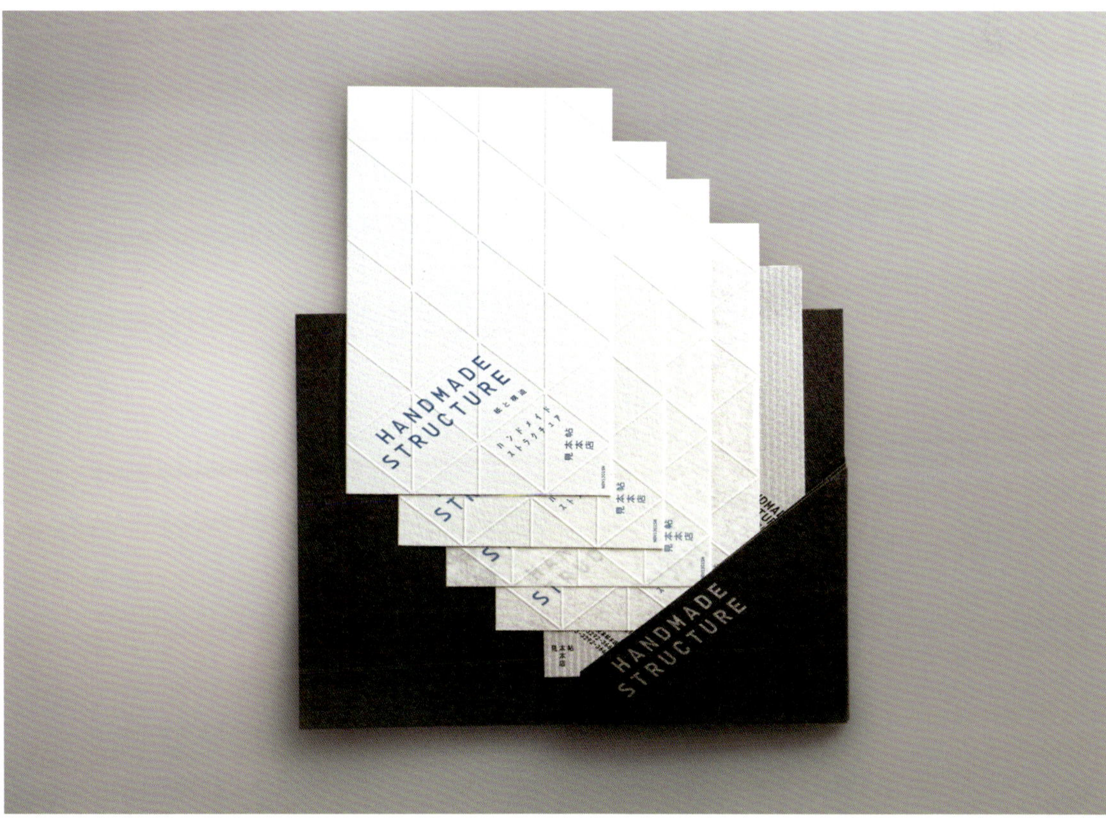
HANDMADE
STRUCTURE

Perception

—Ágnes Herr

For a personal project that expresses Ágnes Herr's idea of optical illusions, this double layer poster transforms with perception. Playing with positive and negative space, "perception" is deconstructed and printed on the base layer. Wavy stripes of changing thickness are printed on a transparent film and placed in front, doubling into a moiré pattern that visually alters "perception" when viewed from different directions.

Effects Screenprinting, non-paper materials

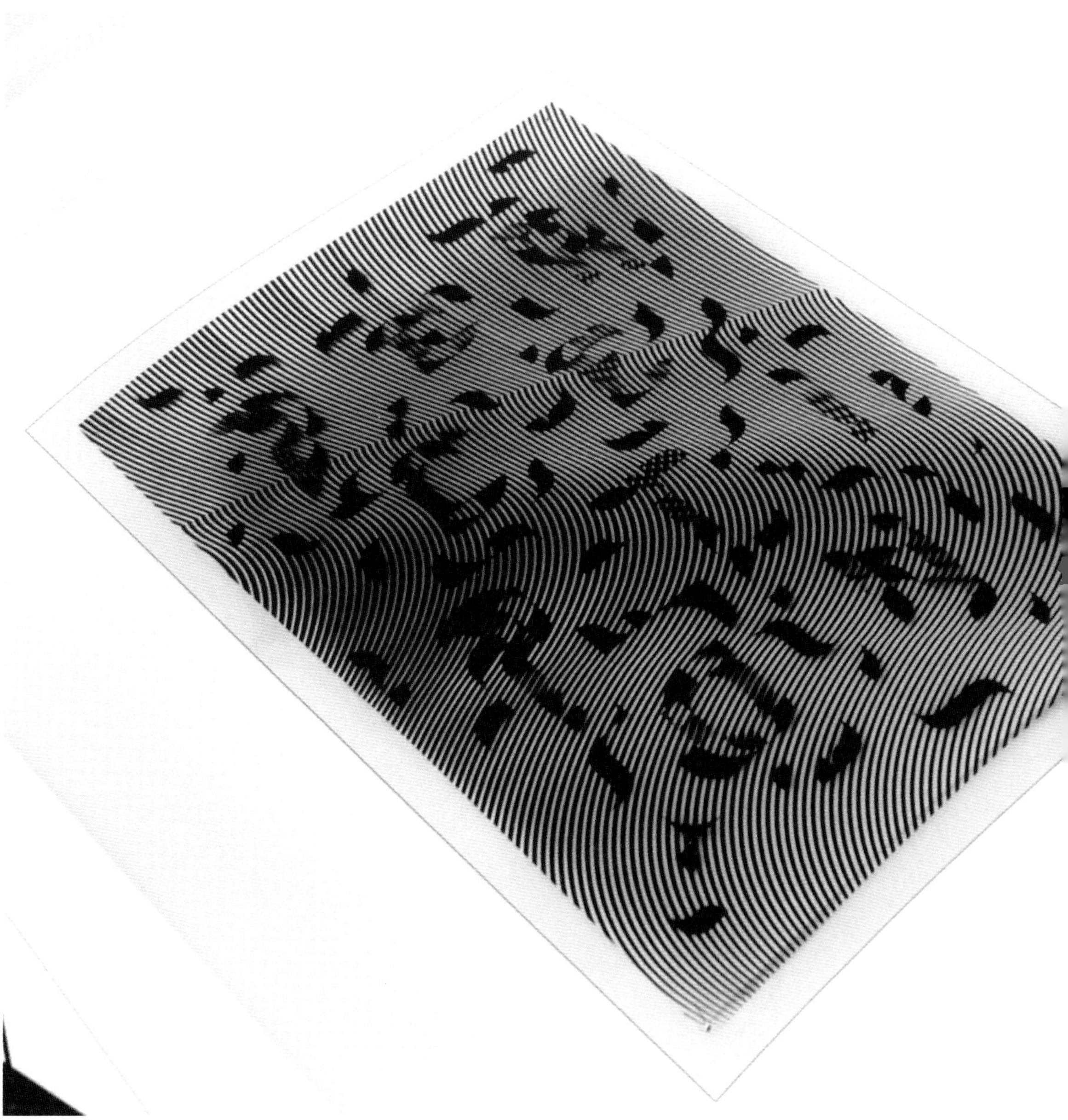

Ingenuity. Nature.

—84000 Communications Limited

Inspired by the success of Taiwanese calligrapher Tong Yang-tse's campaign to highlight the possibilities of calligraphy at present, these posters invited the public to write directly on them using simply water to reveal strokes. Made of a velvet that can trace water contact and quickly recover as it blots up the fluid, the posters enabled repeated exercises, the same way school kids used to practice calligraphy generations ago. With only a small seal script saying "I see", "I write" and "I think", the designer removed himself from the posters and let participants be the subject.

Client Company Asian Culture and Arts Development Association
Effects Non-paper material

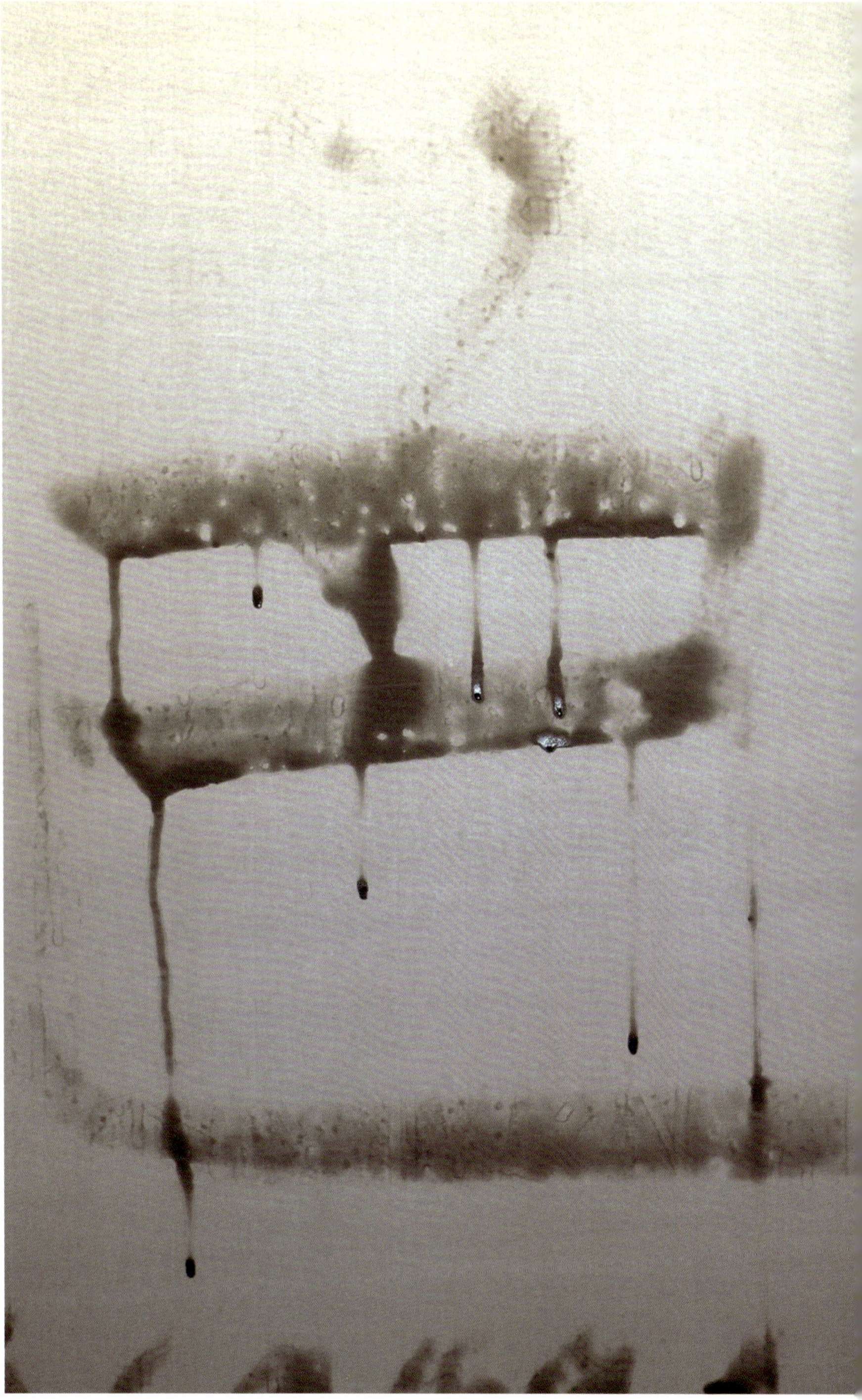

German Flood Relief Poster

—ONOGRIT

After Germany experienced massive floods in June 2013, ONOGRIT wanted to draw more public attention to the tragedy. To elicit vivid memories of the floods, they created a series of posters, all individually treated and dipped in mud water, allowing each to appear slightly different and illicit for a more personal feeling. The neon pink headline TEIL' DEIN GLÜCK means, "Share your fortune".

Special credits Sascha van den Bloock, Ruth Biniwersi
Effects Screenprinting

HELFEN IST FREUNDSCHAFT. FREUNDSCHAFT IST
- HOCHWASSER 2013 -

TEIL' DEIN GLÜCK
TEIL' DEIN GLÜCK

Pop Up Lokal

—LWZ

Created for a pop-up restaurant as the theme of a semester project at the Vienna University of Technology's 2012, the 100x70cm poster has every detail laser cut. No part of it was printed. The posters have different colours of background, visible through cut out details of people, trees, streets and buildings that pop up individually.

Client Architectural department of the Technical University Vienna
Laser cutting Daniel König
Production buero bauer
Stencil Igor Labudovic
Effects Laser cutting

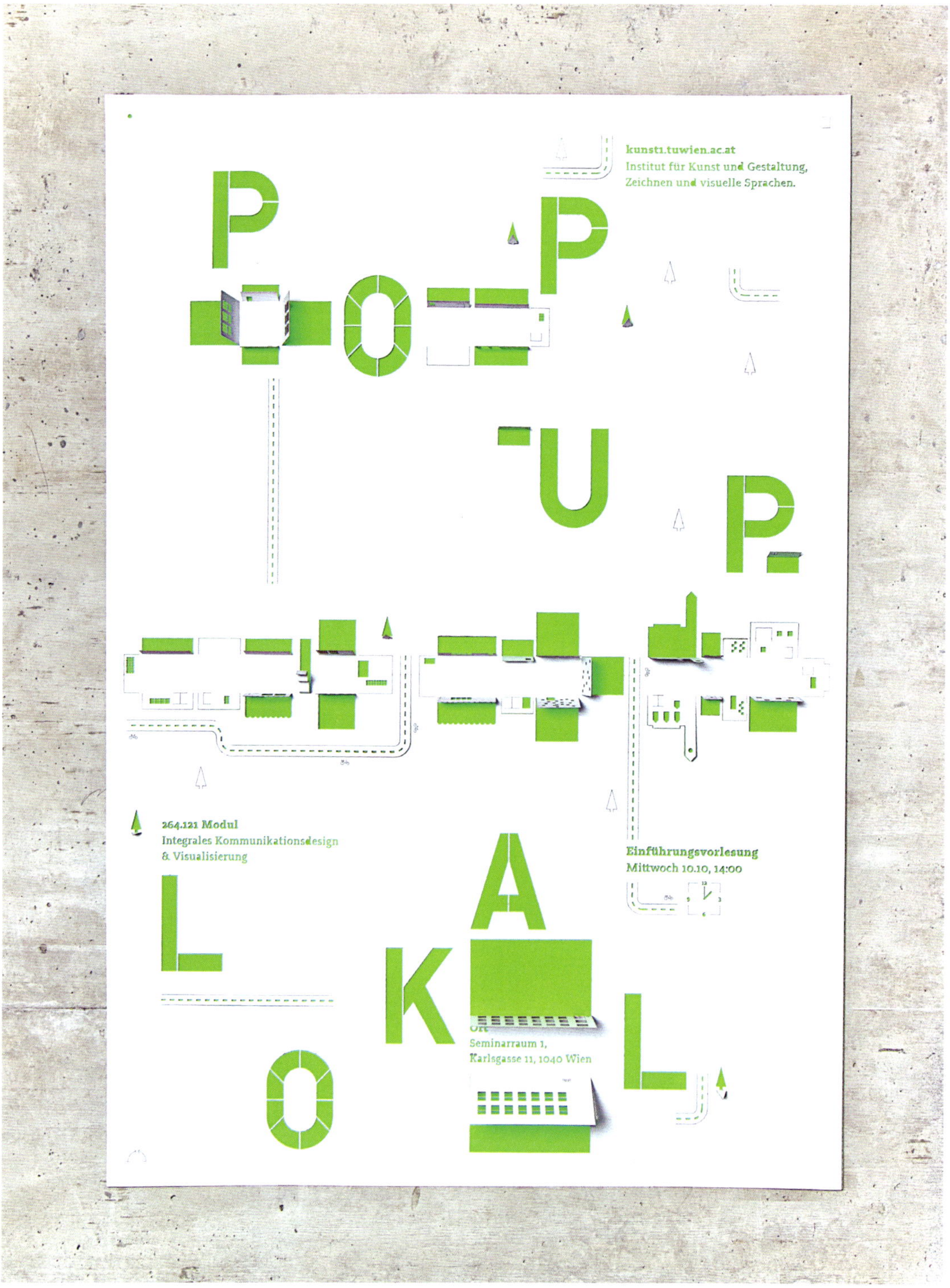

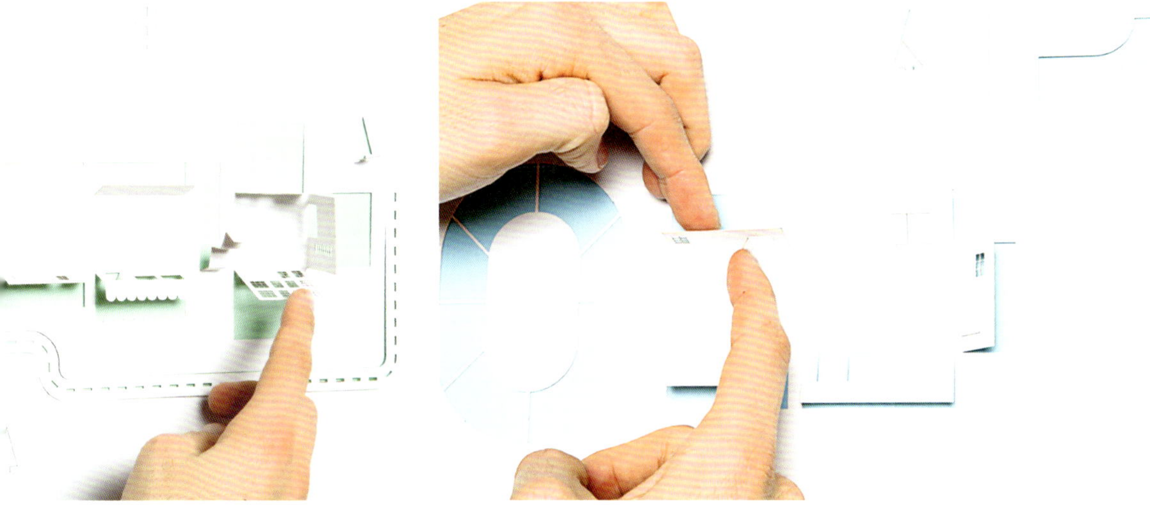

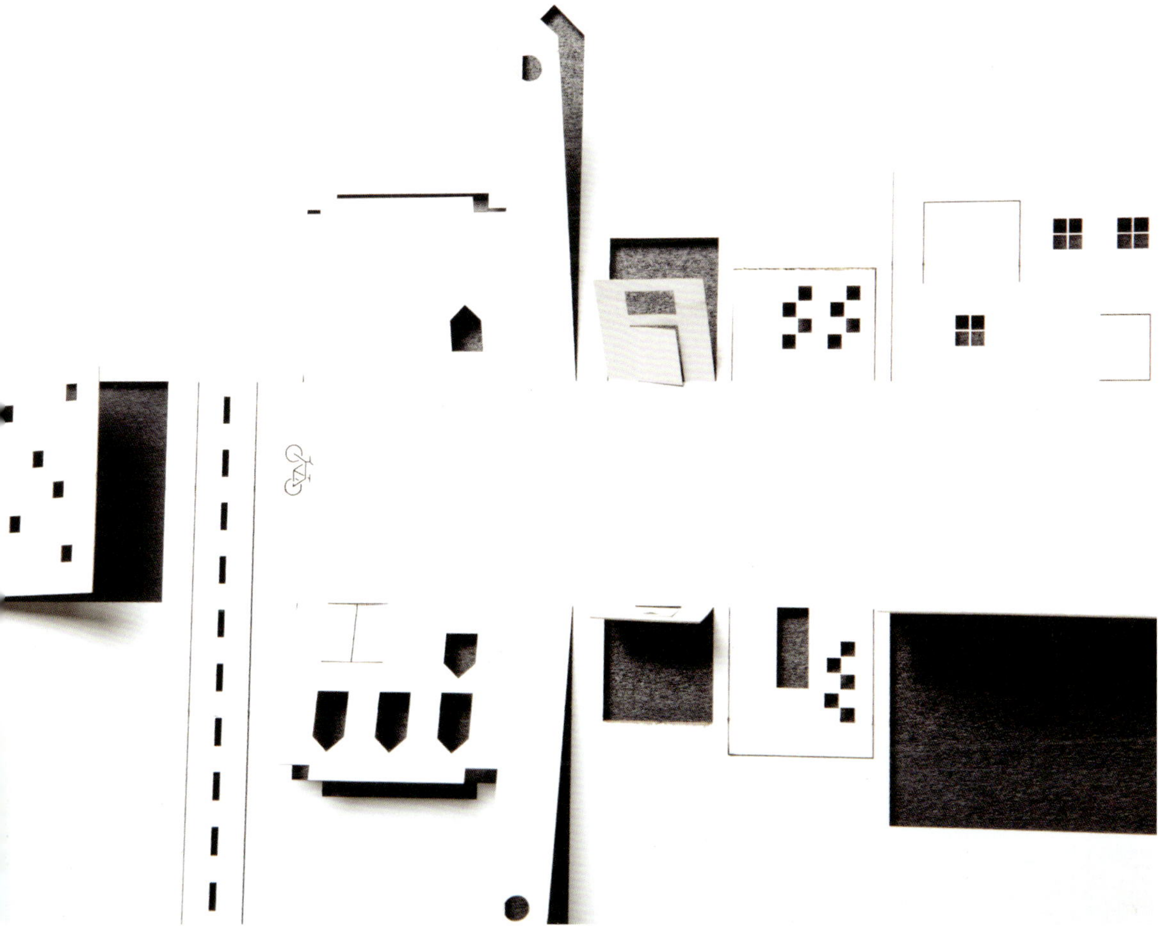

COMMUNE Winter Greeting

—COMMUNE

By using a chunky double sided postcard, COMMUNE inserted a movie flip book that advertised the company for their 2012 winter greeting. On the reverse of the flip book, imagery of the company's portfolio will become visible. To reveal the content, simply rip open the sealed postcard. The flip book can be unfolded like an accordion, and when it's fully opened, a double-sided poster can be seen.

Effects Technical folding, spot colour

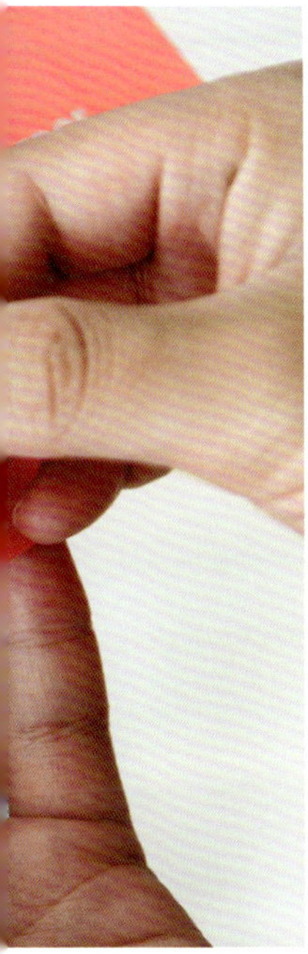

Kaleidoskoop

—AKU

Catching the eyes with a delicate dome, these limited edition 3D posters were specially made to celebrate the fifth birthday of Kaleidoskoop club night. The designer has wished to incorporate spatial elements in the conventionally flat posters. The result is a size A2 poster with a coral crêpe paper decoration that reflects diversity of the club's music and the people.

Client Kaleidoskoop club night
Effect Technical folding

KALEIDOSKOOP
«5 AASTAT TÄIS»
LAUPÄEV 17.12
KL 23–05
KUKU KLUBI
PÄÄSE 5 €
ERIK MORNA
VILLU KRAAN
DRUMMIE/ORAV
+
YO FRANKIE! VIDEOINSTALLATSIOON

ANA Masters of Marketing 2012

—Leo Burnett, Dept. of Design

Co-hosted by Leo Burnett, Adweek, and Gannett, the 2012 ANA Masters of Marketing dinner was celebrated with "Less blah more ah". Through blind embossing a collage of hand script typography, Leo Burnett designed a blanched invitation with kaleidoscopic texture. All of the "ahs" amidst the "blahs" are highlighted with pearl white spot varnish to acknowledge the theme.

Client Leo Burnett, Dept. of Design
Effects UV varnishing, hot stamping, letterpress, edge dipping

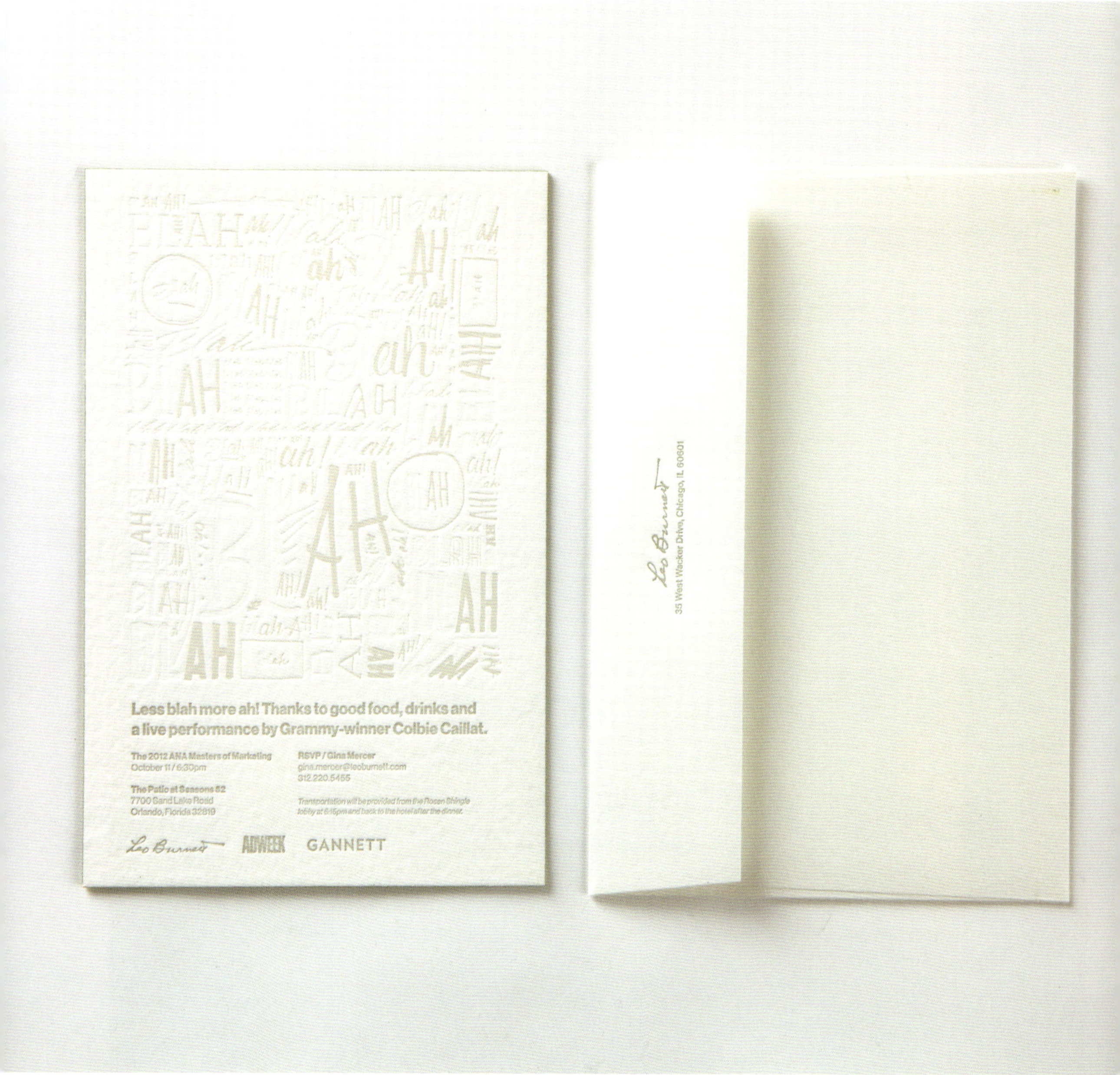

Less blah more ah! Thanks to good food, drinks and
a live performance by Grammy-winner Colbie Caillat.
GANNETT

New Year Card 2011

—Naonori Yago

Naonori Yago's 2011 New Year card is a futuristic paper doll that only takes shape with the help of the recipient. Die cut in an organic shape with a tessellation pattern, one needs to trace the lines to pull off pieces of puzzle one by one. The result is a lovely silhouette breaking away from geometric debris to celebrate the year of rabbit.

Client Original art work
Effects Die cutting

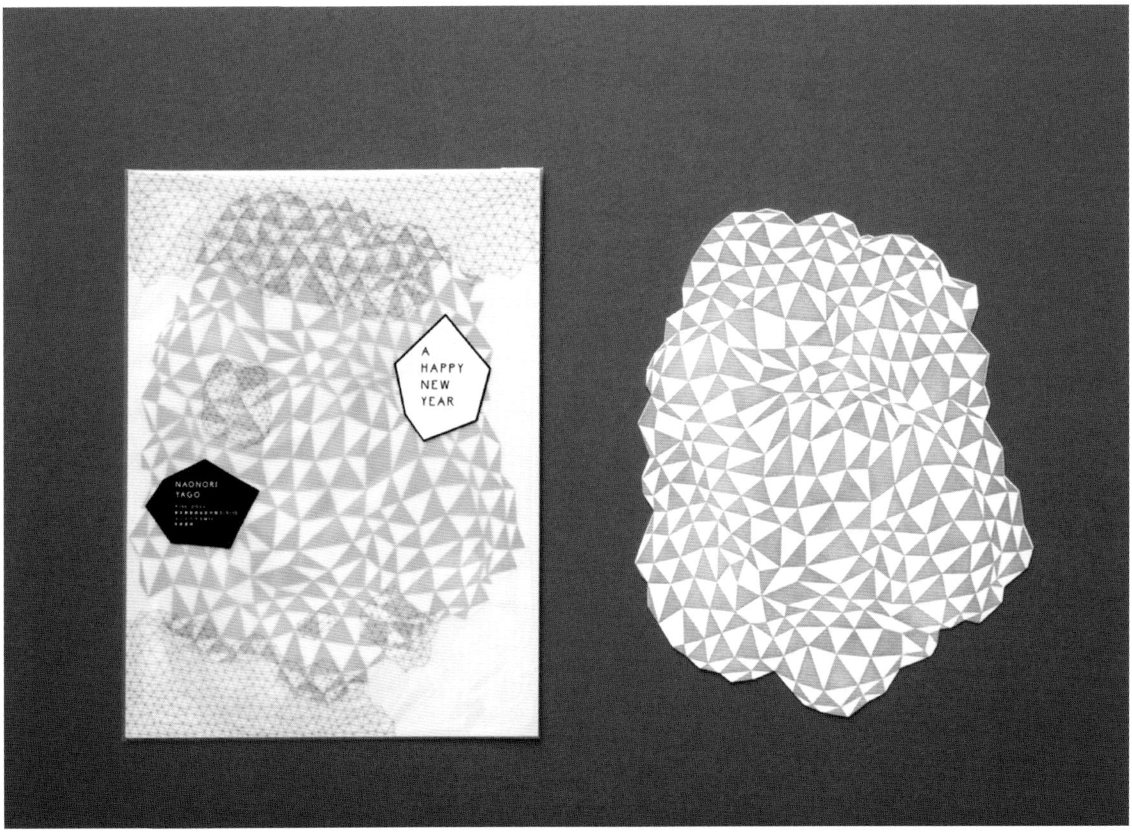

Bynd Artisan

—&Larry

Established by one of Singapore's oldest bookbinders, Bynd Artisan is a retailer and atelier of leather-crafted accessories and stationery. Their heritage and expertise were underlined by a comprehensive set of brochure, poster and postcard. Where the hand-bounded brochure showcases the shop's product and creativity with an assortment of tactile paper and coloured threads, the oversized posters present artisans through a medley of traditional bookbinding supplies, workshop's leftover leather patches and paper scraps. Featuring graphic elements within letters, the postcards were a tribute to the intricacies of the atelier's craftsmanship and bringing its brand ethos of "Something's Worth Sharing".

Client Bynd Artisan
Effects Die cutting, technical folding, spot colour, hot stamping, letterpress, screenprinting, technical binding

THE GOODS:
HONESTY & FINESSE, EMBODIED
Beautifully made and fit for its purpose; Bynd Artisan believes in the enduring qualities of the products we make and it begins with the intentions of our team of craftsmen. Is the paper of the right weight? Does its origins satisfy the concerns of informed customers? Is the tactility of the leather complementary to the structure and stitching?
These are the kinds of questions that we answer in designing every product. When you behold them, all you see is the certainty that our best efforts are ready to be shared with you for a lifetime.
BYND ARTISAN

THE ONE-OFFS:
LET'S MAKE IT YOURS ALONE
Beyond a discreet monogram or a favourite colour, Bynd Artisan is pleased to share with those who desire things uniquely made to their tastes and needs. A team of dedicated craftsmen are ready to design and tailor to your requirements, right here in the atelier.
In a matter of minutes, a handcrafted, one-off notebook made possible through any combination of fine papers, cover materials, stitching and bindings can be in your hands. While special orders with custom leather and letterpress designs may take more time, those who enquire early will find them well worth the wait.
BYND ARTISAN

More than anything, Bynd Artisan is a tribute to the enduring excellence of a small band of professionally trained local craftsmen. In today's world, it is rare to find individuals who would dedicate themselves to the rigours of apprenticeship, be it for bookbinding or leatherwork.
Yet here are three who have invested themselves and earned the rare satisfaction of creating the master designs for beautiful and tangible things in a time of digital fleetingness. It is our privilege to support them and share their works with you.
THE ARTISANS:
A LEGACY SHAPED BY HANDS
BYND ARTISAN

THE COMPANY:
BOUND BY AN ENDURING VISION
The roots of Bynd Artisan can be traced back to 1942, when our original founders started a humble bookbinding shop in Mohamed Sultan Road. It was an honest trade that served a genuine need and the company flourished by being skilled at it through the decades.
The way they saw it, a book well made meant that people could entrust whatever they treasured to its pages, to be shared or returned to as desired. This remains true today, even as we continue to hone our craft and seek out better methods and materials with which to continue earning that trust.
ORIGINAL HEIDELBERG
BYND ARTISAN

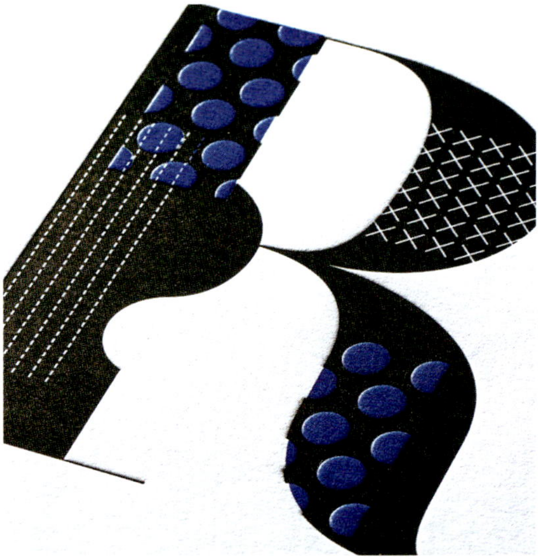

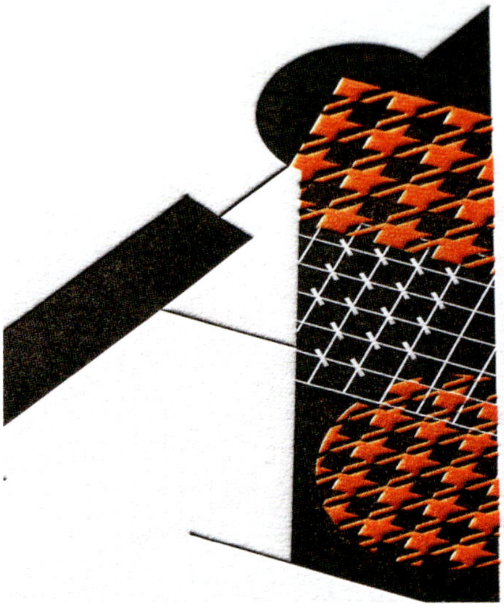

Bocuse d'Or Asia Pacific 2014

—artless Inc.

artless Inc., Japan, has designed the menu for their home team for the Asia Pacific round of Bocuse d'Or, a biennial world chef championship. Chef Hideki Takayama's culinary creation is presented with a slender accordion fold on traditional washi paper, topped with a full moon blind-embossessed as a tactile emblem of traditional Japanese beauty. The moon theme extended to the interior in the colour of silver.

Client Maison de Gill Ashiya
Creative direction Junji Tanigawa, JTQ Inc.
Photo Kenichi Yamaguchi
Effects Embossing

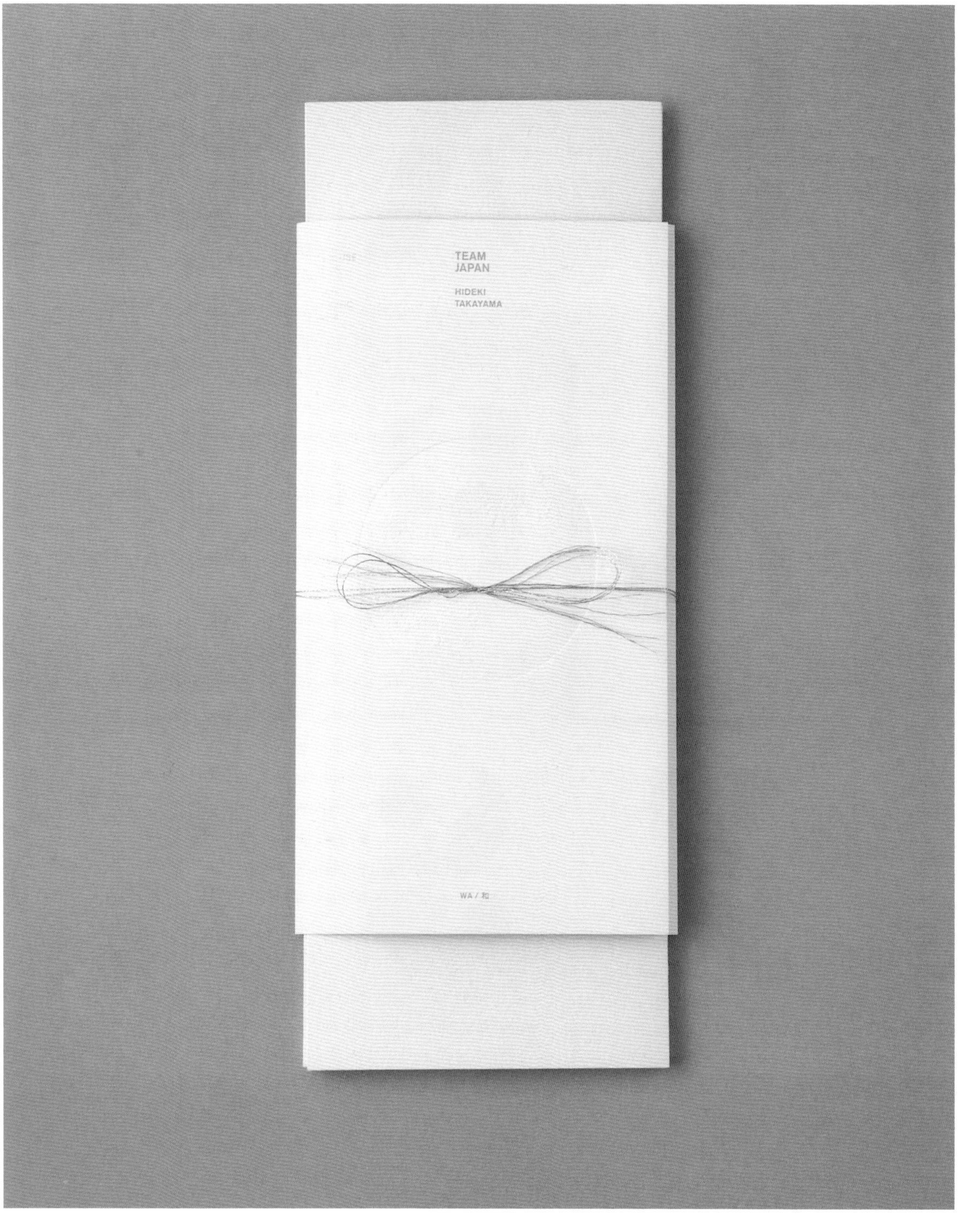

MEAT

MEAT

HIDEKI
TAKAYAMA

Specials Applied from G.F Smith

—StudioMakgill

From blind debossing and lithography to foiling and die cutting, Specials Applied is a meticulous matching of print and finishing effects that brings the most out of G.F Smith's select specialty paper. Details of paper texture, colour and shine are narrated by the paper company's new G.F Smith Bold typeface, bringing itself closer to the UK's design studios and printers through its designed-oriented presentation.

Client G.F Smith
Printing Benwells
Effects Die cutting, hot stamping, debossing, letterpress, duplex

Specials
Applied
from G F Smith

ISBA 2013

—UMA/design farm

For the 2013 International Symposium on Single Biomolecule Analysis, UMA/design farm extracted an image from the hosting city, Kyoto, to form the basis of the flyer and poster design. The text colour changes when cut across by yellow and white stripes. Inspired by one of the study's special analytical ways to utilise voltage, the diagonal colour blocks on the flyer are enhanced by folding.

Client OSAKA UNIVERSITY, Support Office for Large-Scale Education and Research Projects
Photo Yoshiro Masuda
Effects Technical folding, debossing

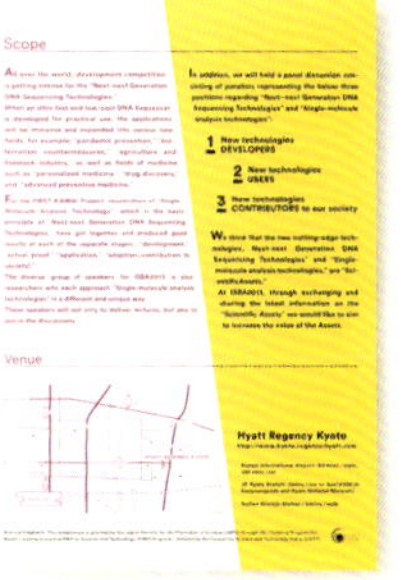

Nano Pore Sequencing :
November
21st (Thu)
22nd (Fri)
2013
Hyatt Regency Kyoto,
Kyoto, Japan
Registration
Entry from our website
Free of charge
Up to 300 Persons
Secretariat of ISBA2013

Third International Design Congress of Catalonia Posters

—Xavi Martínez

To Xavi Martínez, the future can be understood as one strange hidden thing — and that strange hidden thing of this poster is its backside Conceived for ESDi's Third International Design Congress of Catalonia, themed "Future Trends", the upcoming schedule was printed on the poster's back to denote "what's to be explored". Customised alignments suggested varied ways of folding that reformed poster design without weakening legibility.

Client ESDi University
Effects Technical folding

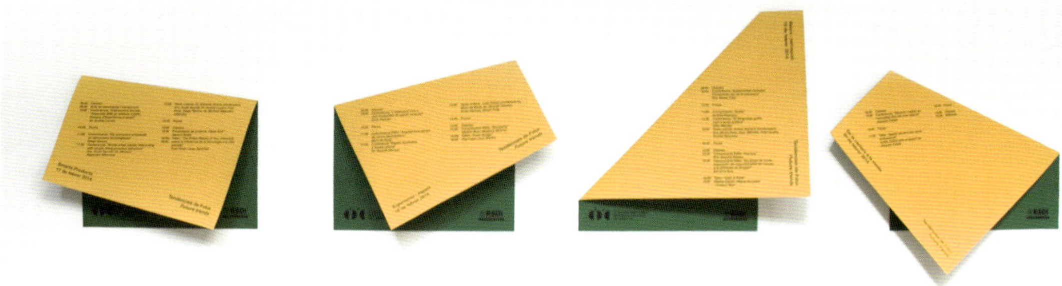

Escola
Superior
ESDi

Tendències de Futur
Future trends
17/18/19/20 de febrer 2014
ESDi

Eduardo Basualdo Exhibition Invitation

—Studio Hausherr

Titled “The End of Ending”, Argentinian artist Eduardo Basualdo’s solo exhibition featured a black sculptural installation that filled the venue to the brim. It leaves interested viewers only one route to circulate this organic object with no goal and no end. By using the same material, Studio Hausherr designed the invitation as an extension of the exhibit, with looping blind embossed show info to resonate the theme.

Client Eduardo Basualdo
Effects Debossing, non-paper materials

Thalassa

—Kanella

Meaning 'sea' in Greek, Thalassa attempts to simulate the work of nature with printing. Available in two versions, the limited edition posters capture the vast sea and the reflection of the sun and moonlight using a split fountain technique. Ink is added every five prints to let the colour darken, creating an impression of the night slowly taking over the day. The design was silkscreened on Munken Pure paper with a 3mm matte white PVC finishing to add a glossy effect. The 'night' edition was made special with a glow-in-the-dark ink.

Effects Special ink, screenprinting

Arjowiggins Creative Papers Christmas Card

—Blast

Grasping the festive spirit, Blast created a set of Christmas card for Arjowiggins, letting the creative paper manufacturer deliver their quality products into the hands of clients and friends. Printed with a "Create Your Christmas" blessing, the direct mail holiday card came complete with multicolour inserts of geometric die cuts where recipients could arrange their bespoke Christmas tree adornment for celebration.

Client Arjowiggins
Printing Gavin Martin Colournet
Effects Die cutting, hot stamping

Products & Packages

Products & Packages

Products & Packages

Products & Packages

Products & Packages

Products & Packages

Products & Packages

Products & Packages

Products & Packages

Handle Recycling

— IYA Studio

IYA Studio worked with Handle Recycling on the latter's branding identity, including the rollout of its packaging, print and digital materials. Inspired by the look created by compressed materials, the team used the fluid forms to inform the brand's visual language. The blend of sans and serif types was also done in the same spirit of repurposing and combining different materials to create something new and unexpected.

Client Handle Recycling Ltd
Product Photography Tian Khee Siong
Effects Die cutting & perforation, folding, hot stamping, debossing

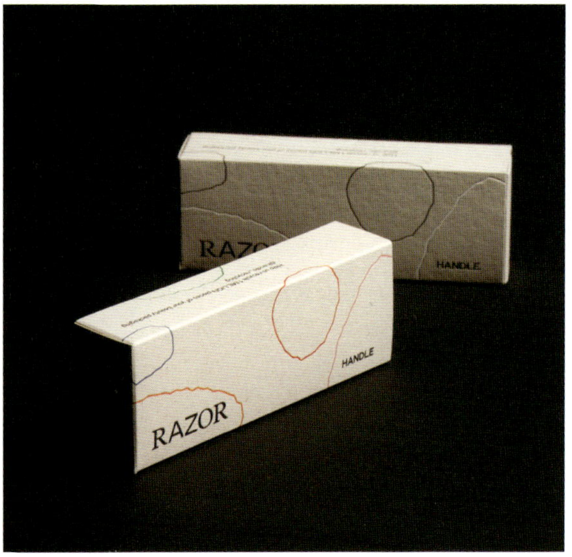

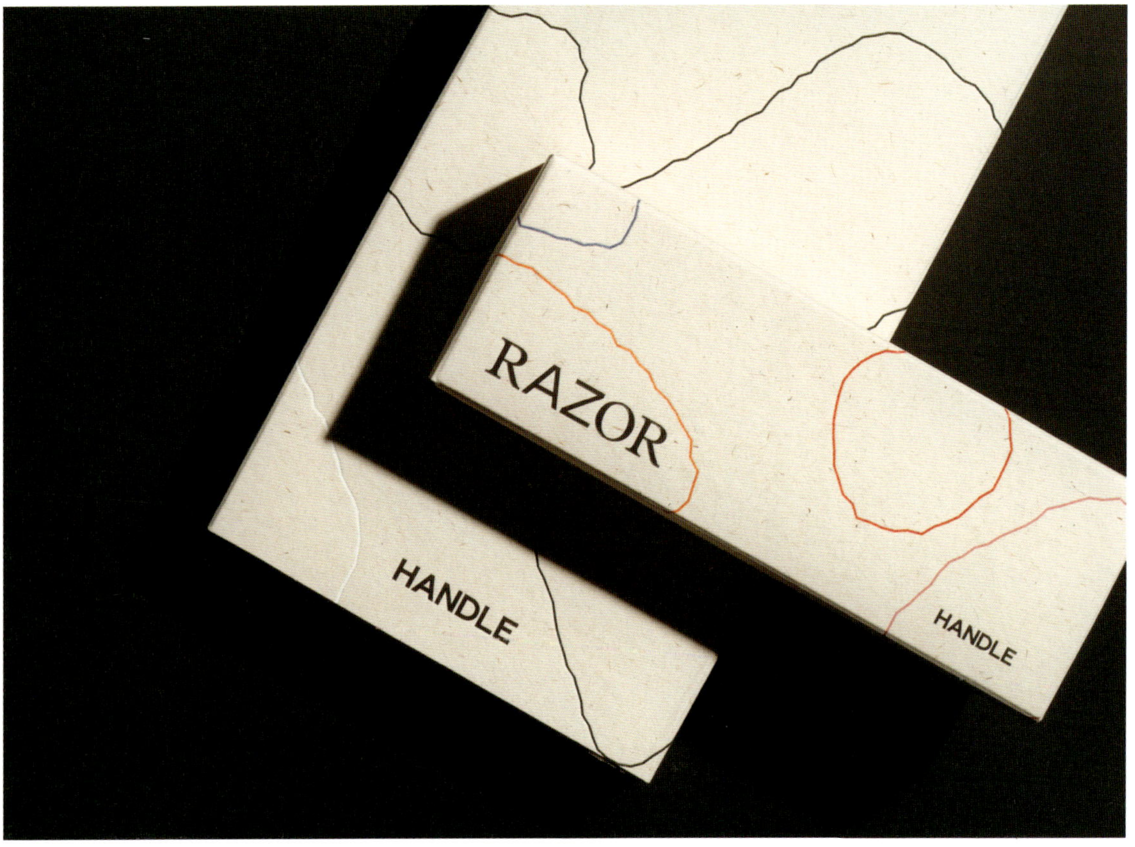

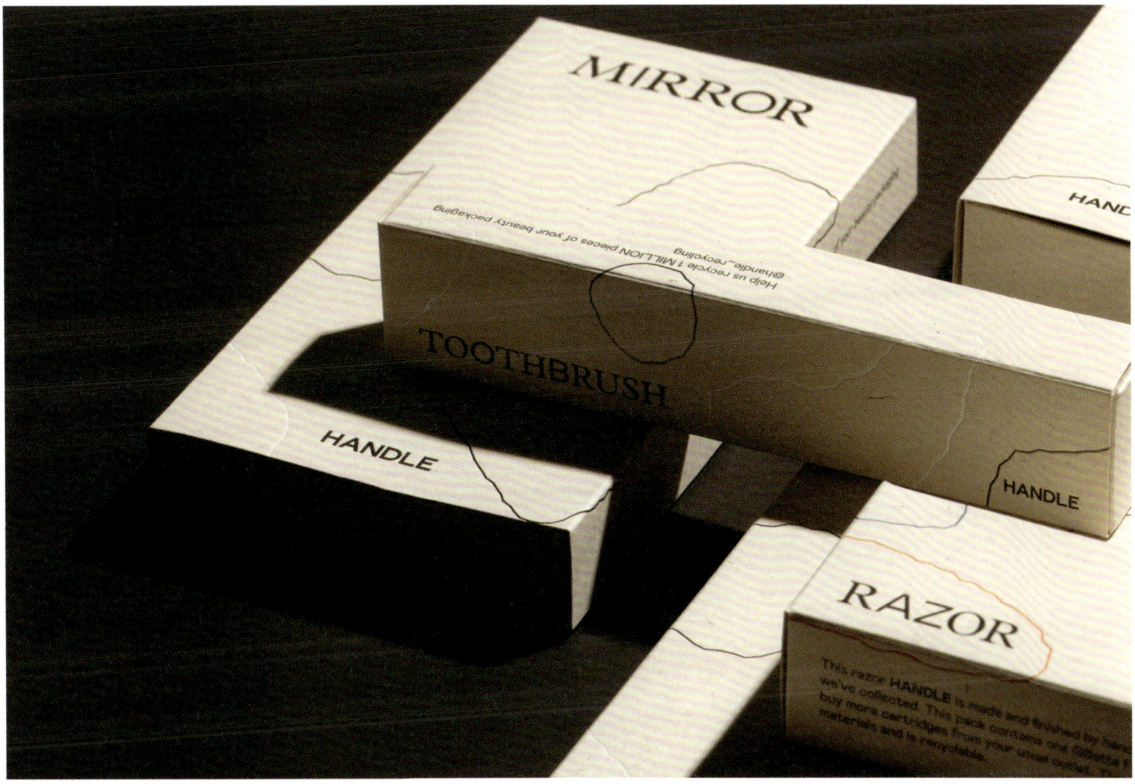
MIRROR
Help us recycle 1 MILLION pieces of your beauty packaging
@handle_recycling
TOOTHBRUSH
HANDLE
HANDLE
RAZOR

RAZOR
HANDLE

We are HANDLE, the recycling company for the Beauty industry
WE NEED YOUR EMPTY PACKAGING!
Discover More @handle_recycling
HANDLE
handlerecycling.com

Gift for Your Beloved

— studiowmw

studiowmw created a unique gift for all occasions through their 'Gift for Your Beloved' red packets. Featuring 24 designs that utilise up to 18 types of quality paper and more than 10 printing effects like hot-stamping, laser cutting and the like, it allows people to receive joy throughout the year rather than just during Chinese New Year. By transforming the packets into gifts, the studio hopes to use the power of design as a way of sustaining a fading culture and extending the product lifespan to new occasions, allowing people to share special blessings anytime.

Client Polytrade Paper
Effects Die cutting & perforation, technical folding, spot colour, UV varnishing, hot stamping, embossing & debossing, laser cutting, screenprinting, non-paper materials

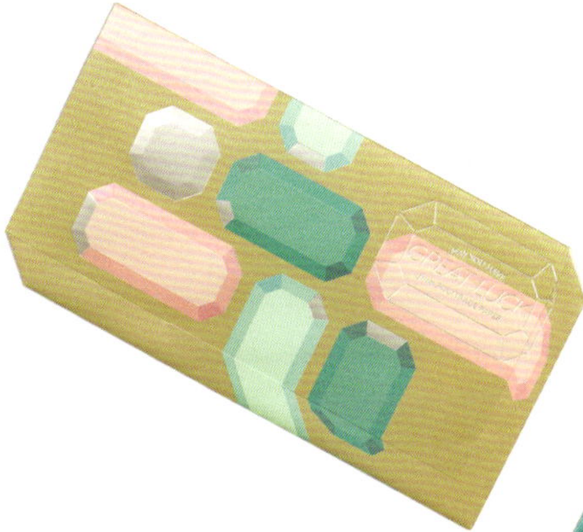

happiness & prosperity

BIG PROFIT
WISH YOU
HAPPINESS & PROSPERITY
From Polytrade Paper
GOOD LUCK

Good Luck
MAY ALL YOUR WISHES COME TRUE
Big Profit

May your business flourish
HAPPINESS & PROSPERITY
Happiness and Prosperity
GOOD LUCK IN THE YEAR
May your business grow and expand
May you have great success in your career
MAY ALL GO WELL WITH YOU
Good health
New aspirations
MAY ALL GO WELL WITH YOU
Happy New Year
Good Health
May your
happiness & pros

your business flourish
happiness & prosperity
Happiness and Prosperity
Good health
New aspirations
GOOD LUCK IN YEAR
May you have GREAT SUCCESS IN YOUR CAREER
MAY ALL YOUR WISHES COME TRUE from POLYTRADE PAPER
MAY ALL YOUR WISHES COME TRUE

Project Charisma

—BLOW

Aptly named "Charisma", reflecting the irresistible charm of femininity and character of Polytrade papers, and acknowledging the uniqueness among both, a bespoke set of effects was used to match eight types of Polytrade paper and create a range of promotional teasers in various forms of cosmetics packaging. This includes a premium box set with eight lip stick packaging, various brightly coloured flyer designs and an eye shadow memo pad as a special gift.

Client Polytrade
Effects Die cutting, technical folding, spot colour, hot stamping, embossing & debossing, screenprinting

PROJECT—
CHARISMA

PROJECT—
CHARISMA
BY
POLYTRADE
PAPER

PROJECT—
CHARISMA

PROJECT—
CHARISMA

Fishion Chinese New Year Pocket

—BLOW

Optimised for printing, Polytrade's scintillating astrobrights papers delivers spectacular visual. To coincide with the lunar New Year, a contemporary set of red pockets was created to efficaciously showcase the papers' distinctive properties. Inspired by fish, 16 designs illustrate the elegant movement of the creature, combined with ultra fine press and metallic foil that produces impressive touches.

Client Polytrade
Effects Die cutting, technical folding, spot colour, UV varnish, hot stamping, embossing & debossing, screenprinting

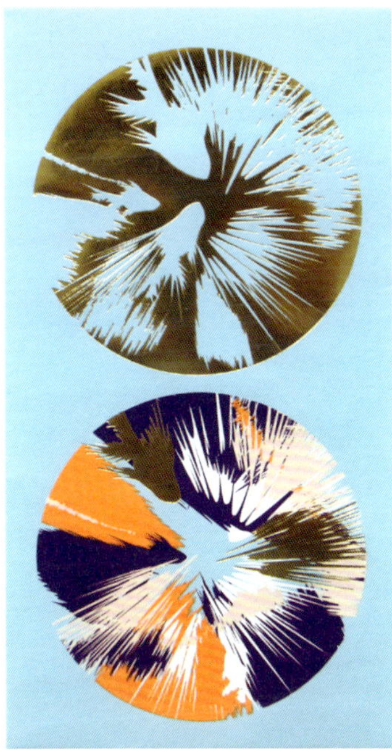

Gorky Park Ice-cream

—Anastasia Genkina

For generations, Gorky Park ice cream has carried a historical charm with its consumers, providing a cool and classic treat in one of Moscow's famous park. To keep a timeless recipe feel modern and relevant, six brightly colour-coordinated patterns were developed for the packaging. Inspired by the park, a place of recreation, fun and play, simple repeating shapes evoke a spirit of endless summer for these ice cream products.

Client Moscow Gorky Park
Art direction Misha Gannushkin
Effects Spot colour

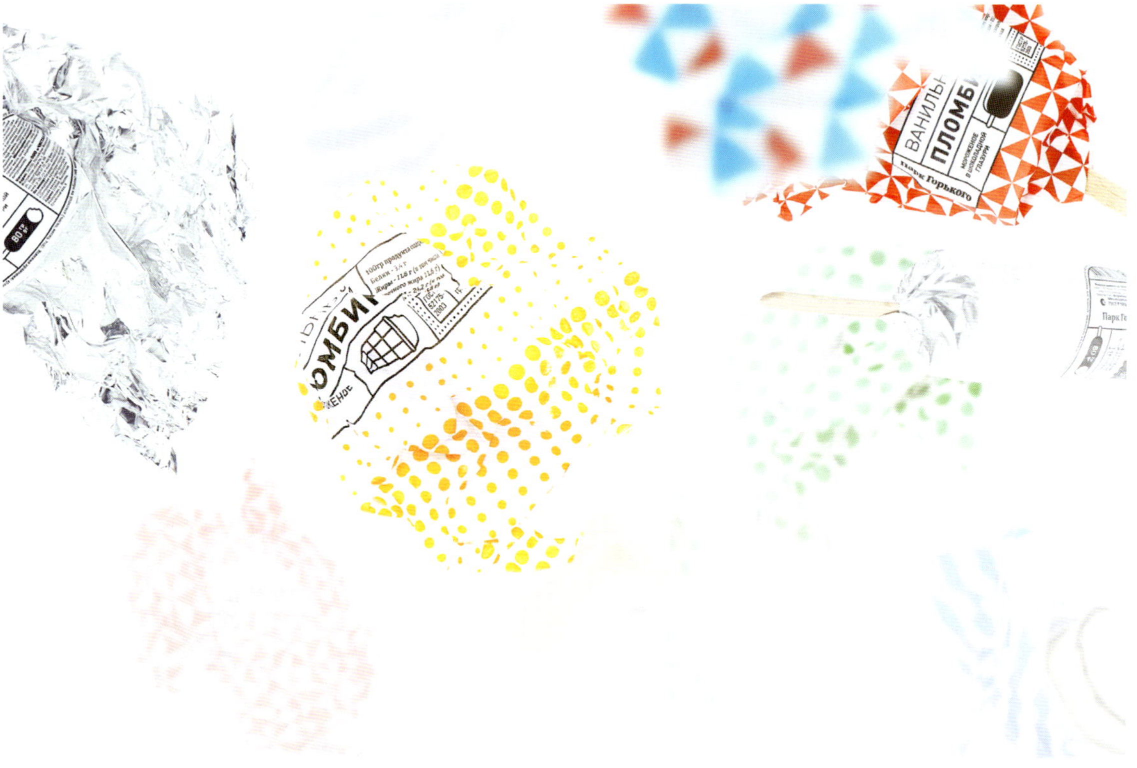

ВАНИЛЬНЫЙ
ПЛОМБИР
МОРОЖЕНОЕ С ШОКОЛАДНОЙ ГЛАЗУРЬЮ

ЭСКИМО
ПЛОМБИР
МОРОЖЕНОЕ В ШОКОЛАДНОЙ ГЛАЗУРИ
Парк Горького

ВАНИЛЬНЫЙ
ПЛОМБИР
МОРОЖЕНОЕ
Парк Горького

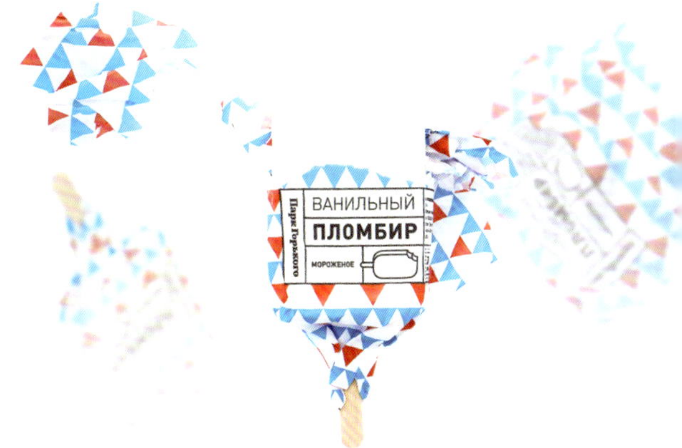
ВАНИЛЬНЫЙ
ПЛОМБИР
МОРОЖЕНОЕ
Парк Горького

ШОКОЛАДНЫЙ
ПЛОМБИР
МОРОЖЕНОЕ

ВАНИЛЬНЫЙ
ПЛОМБИР
МОРОЖЕНОЕ В ШОКОЛАДНОЙ ГЛАЗУРИ
Парк Горького

Парк Горького
ГЛАЗУРИ
80 гр
gr
ГОСТ Р 52175-2003

Парк Горького
ШОКОЛАДНЫЙ
ПЛОМБИР
МОРОЖЕНОЕ
100 г содержат
Жиры 24,4г
Белки 3,4г
Углеводы 3,4г
319,5 ккал

Rice Creative x Marou Opening Invitation & Gift

—Rice Creative

Rice Creative believes rice and bowl together impart prosperity. For their new office opening, a party invitation was briefly folded into a paper bowl, blind embossed with a map and messages in true fortune cookie copywriting style, and finished off with their new company chop. The party gift was a custom-made, hand numbered crisped rice chocolate bar, especially made by Rice's long-term partner and client, Marou. In an edition of 50, each bar is wrapped in a "white tuxedo" paper, with the story of their collaboration impressed at the back.

Photo Wing Chan
Effects Technical folding, embossing

RICE CREATIVE
193 LE THANH TON
D.1, HO CHI MINH

0000001

MAROU & RICE CREATIVE

Paper Brick

—nendo

These three-dimensional looking tricolour blocks play with shade and perspective. 3D-CAD can create three-dimensional forms on a two-dimensional screen surface. This toy translates the concept of 3D-CAD into analogue form through a puzzle that can be played by creating one large cube. Since it's actually a 2D design, there is no chance of the cube collapsing, allowing people to play with gravity defying designs.

Client Pen
Photo Ayao Yamazaki
Effects Laser cutting

Sticker Calendar

—nendo

This offset printed daily peel away sticker calendar reveals the scenery of the forthcoming season, as calendar days are removed bit by bit, day after day. Where festive occasions, like Valentine's Day or Christmas days, are marked by special illustrations, pictures develop into a meaningful story that corresponds to the day. A whimsical cat is hidden at random spots on each page, making the peeling process much more fun.

Client by | n
Photo Akihiro Yoshida
Effects Die cutting

11
12
11
12
11
12

1
2
1
2
1
2
5
6

9
10
9
10
9
10

5
6
6

7
8
7
8
7
8

Land Rover Topographic Calendar

—Zeynep Orbay

Land Rover's 2014 daily calendar is a 3D version of a topographic map. Each level represents a month that has its own Pantone colour and is die cut using a different blade. The number on the edge of every page shows the remaining days of the year.

Client Land Rover
Agency TBWA Istanbul (İlkay Gürpınar, Zeynep Karakaşoğlu, Zeynep Orbay)
Effects Die cutting, spot colour, screenprinting

1 JANUARY
LAND ROVER TOPOGRAPHIC
CALENDAR

2 JANU

Enchantment by Lu, Wei

—Aaron Nieh Workshop

Embroidery, hot stamping and stitch binding intertwine in this project, evoking a tranquil serenity akin to Taiwan's east coast. For Lu, Wei's album "Enchantment", the night sky, islands and ocean come together conveying fragments of the region's human culture, all captured as a dialogue with time. The C-fold pamphlet inside completes the visual story as more art is revealed.

Client Luz Chung, Lu wei
Effects Die cutting, technical folding, spot colour, UV varnish, hot stamping, technical binding, non-paper materials

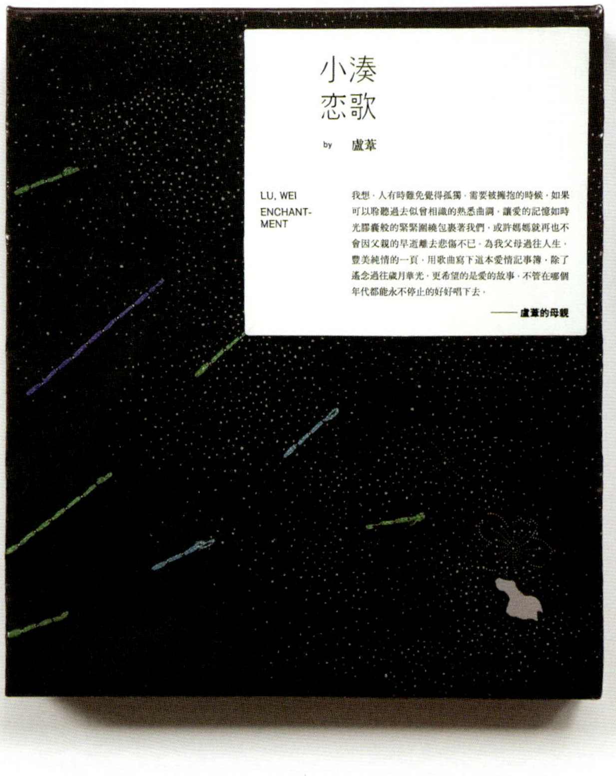

小湊村歌 01. KOMINATO...3'45
手心的浪花 02. SEA SPRAY...3'41
海月 03. MOONLIGHT DANCE...0'32
新港小調 04. THE BALLAD OF HSIN GANG (vocal)...2'21
小豐田村 05. THE OL' HAMLET...3'56
比西里岸 06. BISILIAN...4'25
到綠島・請寫信 07. SONGS MY TEACHER TAUGHT ME (vocal)...3'03
浪煙 08. EASTERN MISTS...4'52
虹(演唱) 09. RAINBOW (vocal)...4'23
勿忘影中人 10. FORGET ME NOT(vocal)...3'51
新港山嵐霧 11. MOUNTAIN MIST...2'36
新港小調 12. THE BALLAD OF HSIN GANG (instrumental)...0'54
勿忘影中人 13. FORGET ME NOT(JAZZ BAND)...4'30
泥巴小路上的扶桑花 14. HIBISCUS (vocal)...3'04

Asking others for a loan, one must swallow his pride. Dad was sensitive to their situation coming from his own desperate past, his compassion ever so evident.
A man once came to our home to settle a debt. He saw me sitting next to our beautiful Yamaha piano and asked " Young lady can you play [The Happy Sailing]"? I replied "No". After the man left Dad said "We can't look down on others with less means or feel their folk songs are inferior". The most successful people would not differentiate. If asked to play Beethoven, you could, and when asked to play [The Happy Sailing] you should.
The lesson my Dad taught me I passed on to my daughter Lu Wei. She learned classical music in Europe, at the same time enjoys K-Pop. She enjoys talking with her Dad about American country rock, and Taiwanese Pop songs. I feel there's no conflict between these genres. A multitude of music styles can only enhance her creativity. Grandpa is elated that she's not particular to only one style of music.
Written by Sheng-hong Wang

MOONLIGHT DANCE
A Young Fisherman

Glowing Calendar

—Graphic design studio by Yurko Gutsulyak

Designed for Russian radar manufacturer Rawenstvo, this Soviet-Russia-format quarterly calendar may look like a piece of mundane office stationery until one turns the light off. Paying homage to Rawenstvo's expertise, six living radars in the shape of mammals glowingly appear across the three flips. Transparent ink has turned a boring office item into a fascinating display after office hours.

Client JSC Rawenstvo
Illustration IC4design
Effects Special ink, laser cutting, screenprinting, non-paper materials

Keong Saik Snacks Press Kit

—Somewhere Else

Secured by an oversized sticker, this takeaway box contained the exciting announcement of Keong Saik Snacks' opening in Singapore. The bistro's laid back environment and blend of Asian and British café culture added a modern twist to classic comfort foods. A pared down design and the mixed alphabets reflected the essence of the new bistro. Also held within the kit was a neat little brand book and a DVD in a French fries-bag like sleeve.

Client Keong Saik Snacks
Effects Die cutting, technical folding, embossing

Opening Menu
KEONG
SAIK
SNACKS

KEONG
SAIK
SNACKS
PRESS RELEASE
PRESS RELEASE
KEONG
SAIK
SNACKS

GMUND Urban

—Paperlux GmbH

GMUND Urban's paper collection is their tribute to urban environments. Overall, warm and dusty colours are used against surfaces such as cement, wood and graphic paper. The hot foil line in copper is the central theme, connecting all the designs together by playing with angles.

Client Büttenpapierfabrik GMUND
Photo Michael Pfeiffer
Effects Die cutting, hot stamping, screenprinting, non-paper materials

Gmund who?
Urban what?
Gmund who?

GMUND
Cement Black
510 gsm
0,7 x 1,0 m
Brasilia Dust
240 gsm
120 gsm

Brasilia Dust
Architect Dust
Sample Book

Cement Grey
Gmund Urban Paper Sample
240 gsm

310 gsm

Urban

110 gsm
0,7 x 1,0 m

Brasilia Dust
250 gsm

Neat Confections

—Anagrama

Specialising in handmade shortbread, Neat Confections is dedicated to creating the taste through organic spices and fruity flavours. Anagrama's solution was to focus consumers' attention on the beautiful biscuits characterised by tantalising colours inspired by the unique ingredients. Where the silver chrome drawer box highlights the food's texture, touches of neon pastel add warmth and lend balance to the sheen.

Client Neat Confections
Effects Die cutting, spot colour, hot stamping

NEAT
CONFECTIONS
TRIBUTO AL GUSTO
UN TRIBUTO AL GUSTO

NEAT
CONFECTIONS
TRIBUTO AL GUSTO
ESTD
2014

NEAT
CONFECTIONS
CAFE MASALA
TE MATCHA

NEAT
CONFECTIONS

Quartz Champagne

—Max Molitor, Cajza Nydén

Two students in Sweden have designed a crafty champagne carrier, preventing the bottle from remaining upright. The design was informed by the notion that champagne is best stored horizontally. In addition to the function of the packaging, it also has a high impact on the shelf, standing out from other products with its geometric folds.

Effects Technical folding, spot colour

QUARTZ
CHAMPAGNE
ÉPERNAY, FRANCE

Alc. By Vol.
375ml
(NM-301279)
ÉPERNAY, FRANCE
QUARTZ
CHAMPAGNE
SEC Stored since: 2005
DOUX Stored since: 2008
BRUT

Polytrade Paper Swatches

—Studio Much

Great Minds On Paper is Polytrade's box set of paper swatches. Techniques such as die cutting and hot stamping were used to make the content of the box set, which includes seven sets of paper swatches and a guide. On the outer packaging, embossing and hot stamping were used to print quotes by great minds such as Georgia O'Keeffe and Vincent Van Gogh.

Client Polytrade
Effects Die cutting, technical folding, spot colour, hot stamping, debossing, non-paper materials

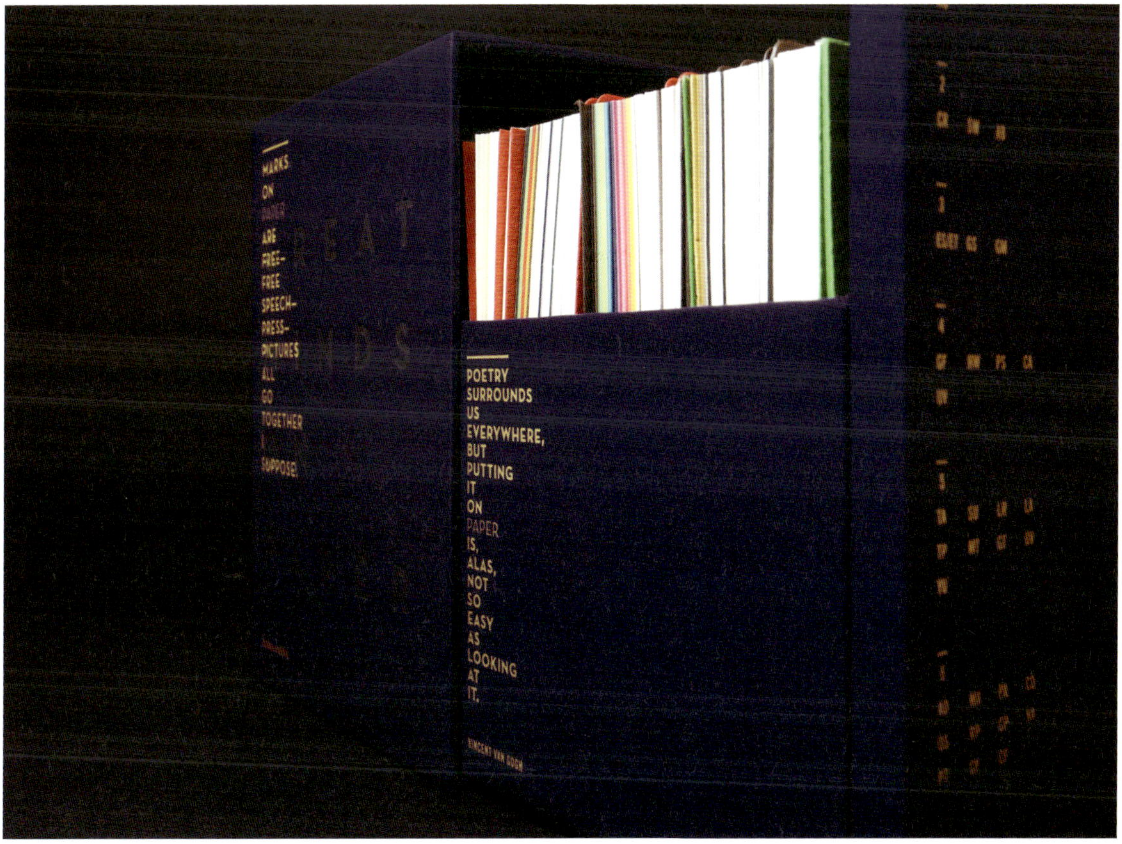
MARKS
ON
PAPER
ARE
FREE-
FREE
SPEECH-
PRESS-
PICTURES
ALL
GO
TOGETHER
I
SUPPOSE.
POETRY
SURROUNDS
US
EVERYWHERE,
BUT
PUTTING
IT
ON
PAPER
IS,
ALAS,
NOT
SO
EASY
AS
LOOKING
AT
IT.
VINCENT VAN GOGH

REFERENCE
GUIDE
GREAT
MINDS
ON
PAPER

Figula Olaszrizling Dűlőválogatás

—Csönge Balla

The soil of the Sóskút Riesling vineyard in Hungary contributes to the fundamental quality of this wine. Overprinted with gold scratch-off paint, the wine label resembles the stratified soil which can be removed as the "topsoil" using the attached Figula commemorative coin and revealing a 'limestone' layer, mimicking the composition of the vineyard's soil. The design was an entry to the Cégér a jó bornak design competition.

Client Cégér a jó bornak design competition
Effects Special ink, hot stamping, non-paper materials

FIGULA OLASZRIZLING DŰLŐVÁLOGATÁS

Promineo White Whiskey

—Chad Michael Studio

From the naming to the packaging design, Promineo is arguably the best demonstration of Chad Michael's branding expertise for premium liquor products. Created as a self-promotional piece with a limited edition of 300, the brand name, Latin for "to stand out", and the whiskey's quality were matched with custom ornate-work pressed onto a Neenah Epic Black paper stock, finished with two engraving inks and two foils. The exclusivity of the project was heightened with bottles that were individually printed, labelled and numbered by hand.

Photo Zachary Goulko
Printing Studio On Fire
Effects Die cutting, hot stamping, non-paper materials

LIMITED RELEASE
BOTTLE NO.
016
YEAR EDITION:
2014
WHISKEY

Promineo
PRODUCT OF NEW YORK

BY THE MAKERS
GENUINE &
SCULPTED
A LIMITED RELEASE OF 300 FROM

ZADOR soap manufactory

—Eszter Laki

A fine bar of Zador soap is infused with botanic essence and healing thermal water from lake Hévíz. Available in seven fragrances, the quality natural ingredients of each fragrance are hand rendered with a brush pen, scanned and edited as ornament and decks the offset printed wrapping paper with Zador emblems. Each soap is hand-wrapped and belted with name of the family manufactory in gold foil.

Client Zador Hungary Ltd
Photo Balázs Glódi
Effects Hot stamping

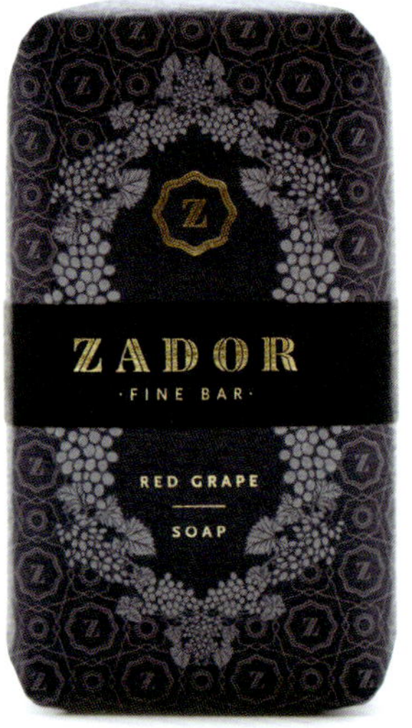

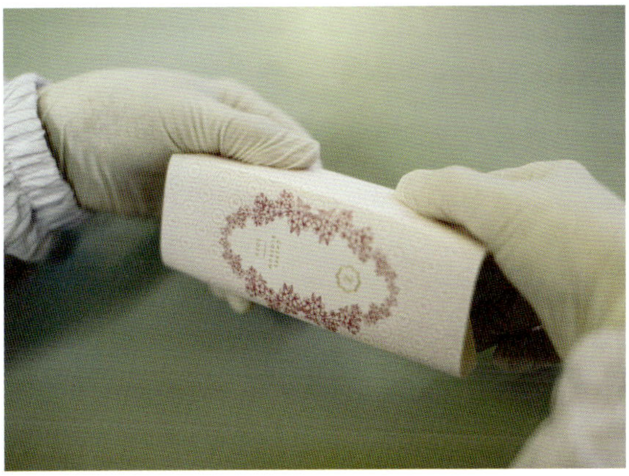

Z
ZADOR
·FINE BAR·

Ivet Fashion Calendar 2014/15

—Four Plus Studio

Comprised of a dozen loose calendar cards, Ivet's Fashion Calendar celebrates the Bulgarian fashion agency's 20th anniversary in 2014. Dates were underlaid by tasteful works of renowned fashion photographer Vasil Germanov, featuring 12 top Bulgarian models in black and white. A sleek golden matte padded envelope wraps the cards, branded with a die-cut sticker that uses a Cyrillic type to underline the agency's long-standing roots.

Client Ivet Fashion
Photo Vasil Germanov
Effects Die cutting, non-paper materials

20 years
Ivet Fashion
model agency
2015

2015

2015
Ivet Fashion
Calendar
ОКТОМВРИ
СЕПТЕМВРИ
АВГУСТ

20 years
Ivet Fashion
model agency
2015

Dávid Borház: DQ

—Csönge Balla

Vineyard and wine merchant Dávid Borház wanted packaging that reflected heritage and place like the carvings of the old mountain, Egerszalók, comprised of rhyolite tuff. Csönge Balla designed labels on grainy paper, representing the rugged walls of the cellar and used perforated stripes to signify the three cellar doors, carved into the volcanic tuff. Once the stripes are torned, stories about the wine, the cellar and the winemaker are revealed.

Client Dávid Borház
Effects Die cutting, letterpress, screenprinting, duplex

A Dávid Borház riolit-tufába vájt mély,
12°C van – ez az átlagos pince-hőmérséklet
így lassan,
fajták 18 hónapig
után 10 hónapig
DÁVID BORHÁZ · DQ · 2011
OLTALOM ALATT ÁLLÓ
Magyar termék
NÉBIH: XXXX

A Dávid Borház riolit-tufába vájt mély,
12°C van – ez az átlagos pince-hőmérséklet
így lassan,
fajták 18 hónapig
a hordásítás után 10 hónapig
DÁVID BORHÁZ
OLTALOM ALATT
Magyar termék
NÉBIH: XXXX
Fiatal borászunk – a borház
rendhagyó megoldásokat. Így
mély tónusú

Arjowiggins x FIAC bookmark

—The Bakery design studio

Every year Arjowiggins collaborates with a design studio to produce a creative bookmark highlighting the quality of its special papers. Making a metaphorical statement for creative practices that require endless exploration and dedication to craft, like mining and fossil extraction, these bookmarks were cut and pressed with a marbling finish like the stone. The bookmarks were given away with the catalogue of the French art festival, FIAC.

Photo Lena Tsibizova
Production Generation Press
Effects Die cutting, hot stamping, embossing, duplex

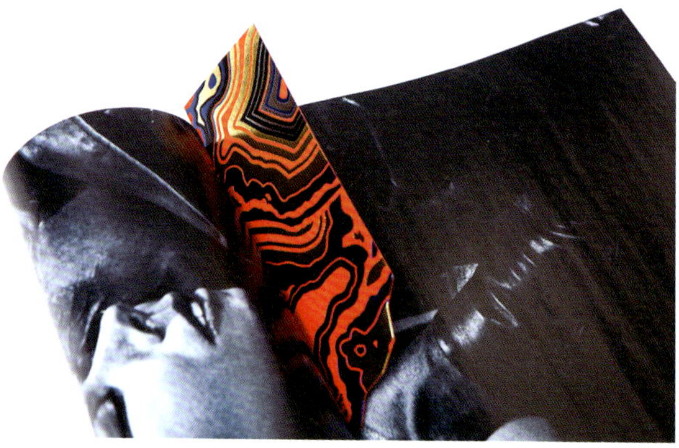

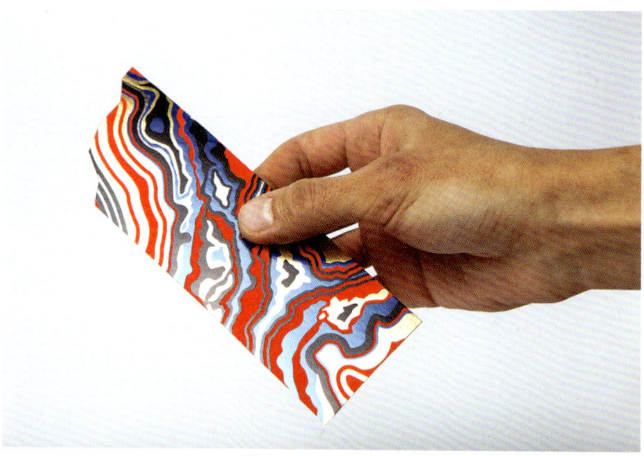

The Cube Calendar

—Philip Stroomberg

Forming a solid cube, 462 paperboard sheets are held together by two binding screws, the calendar designed by Philip Stroomberg is an artful interpretation of the traditional tear-off calendar. Sometimes a date, sometimes a quote about time, the tabs are torn off row after row allowing time to shape this compact object. The Cube Calendar is packaged in a box that retains it shape through folds, negating the need for adhesive.

Production Drukgoed & paardekooper display
Paper Igepa Nederland B.V.
Effects Die cutting & perforation, technical binding, non-paper materials

Time moves
in one
direction,
memory in
another.
William Gibson
September

31
Friday
May

6
Monday
May
5
The Cube
Calendar 2013

MS EUROPA 2

—Paperlux GmbH

Paperlux GmbH designed a lavish invitation for the christening of ocean liner MS Europa 2. In the corporate colour palette of navy, vermilion and white, this typography-led set is enchanted by bizarre maritime vaudeville motifs that appear on the save the date poster with a lustrous Iriodin finish for festivity. They also star in the enclosed paper theatre developed with set designer Tim John, which can be set in motion by a crank found inside the reminder card.

Client Hapag-Lloyd Cruises
Photo Michael Pfeiffer
Effects Die cutting, spot colour, hot stamping, laser cutting, screenprinting, non-paper materials

Todos Somos Niños

—Enserio

Meaning 'we're all children', Girona-based rock band Caiko's first album Todos Somos Niños features a striking image composed by small punctures. The album title and a skull are manually perforated on a white poster that folds into an album cover. Enclosed with a pin pusher, the record was produced with only 200 limited edition copies.

Client Caiko
Video production Caiko
Effects Perforation

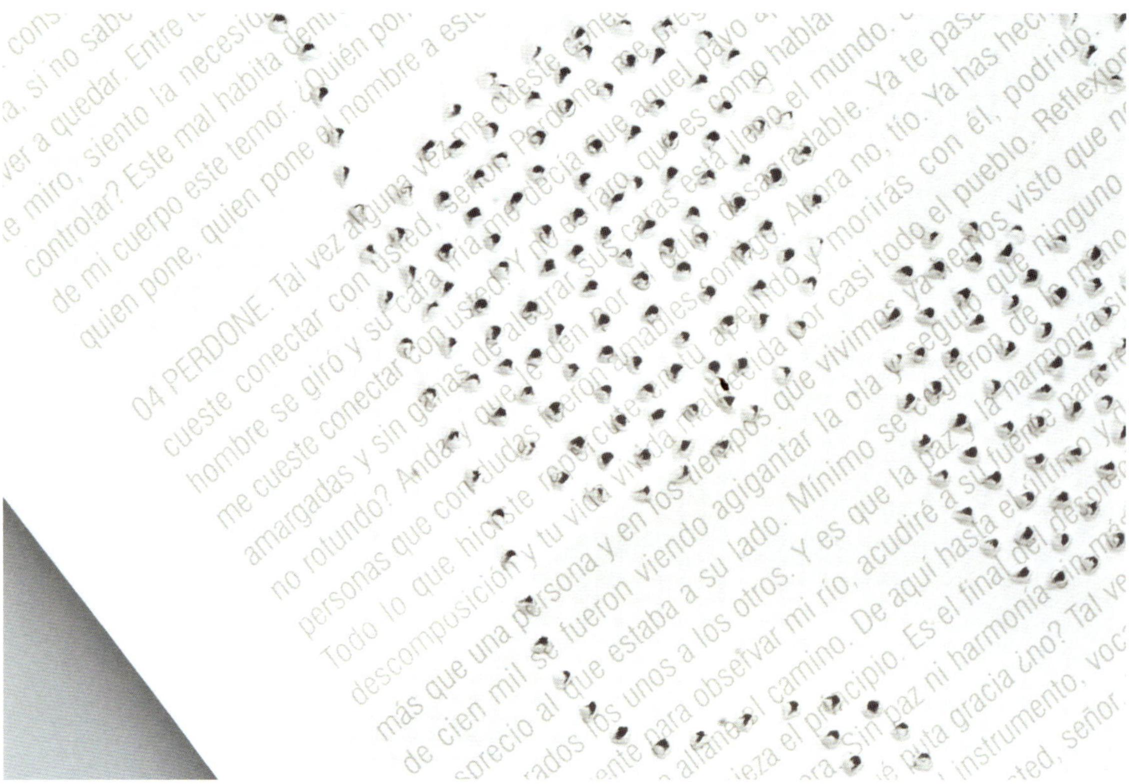

CAIKO
TODOS
SOMOS
NIÑOS
HASTA
QUE
MORIMOS

Basically, books were a luxury item before the printing press.

Nate Silver

CONTRIBUTORS

.Oddity Studio / &Larry / 84000 Communications Limited / A Beautiful Design / Aaron Nieh Workshop / ACST Design / ADDA Studio / Ágnes Herr / AKU / Alexia Roux / Anagrama / Anastasia Genkina / Anonymous / artless Inc. / Asylum / Balmer Hählen / Blast / BLOW / Bratus / Brian Gartside / Bruketa&Zinic OM / Buenos días, / Bureau Hardy Seiler / Bureau Rabensteiner / Büro North / Carlos Bermúdez, Mau Morgó / Chad Michael Studio / COMMUNE / Csönge Balla / Demian Conrad Design / DENTSU INC. / DENTSU INC. CHUBU / Edited / Enserio / Eszter Laki / Éva Valicsek / Firebelly Design / Foreign Policy Design Group / Four Plus Studio / Graphic design studio by Yurko Gutsulyak / Happycentro / Hey / IYA Studio / Jin Ping Soh / Kanella / Kuan-li Tang, Cavis Huang, Jhih-ting Chen / LENS ASSOCIATES INC. / Leo Burnett, Dept. of Design / Lundgren+Lindqvist / LWZ / MAAN Design Studio / Manual / MARKS / Marton Borzak / Max Molitor, Cajza Nydén / mistroom / Mubien / Naonori Yago / nendo / NOSIGNER / Oddds / ONOGRIT / OUWN / Paperlux GmbH / Philip Stroomberg / Power-nap Over / Raw Color / Rice Creative / Somewhere Else / Studio Hausherr / Studio Much / studioKALEIDO / StudioMakgill / studiowmw / The Bakery Design Studio / The Folks Studio / UMA/design farm / viction workshop ltd. / Xavi Martínez / Zeynep Orbay / Zuzanna Rogatty

Biography

.Oddity Studio

.Oddity Studio are a new-wave team of designers and developers in Hong Kong driven by ideas that navigate the creative process beyond trends and despite standards, leading to an impactful outcome above all.

PP. 012-013, 022-025

&Larry

Whether commercial or experimental, &Larry approaches each project with a desire to create works that are honest, functional and expressive beyond aesthetics. The studio has adopted the Eames motto of "take your pleasure seriously" and this philosophy can be seen in a diverse body of work.

PP. 196-199

84000 Communications Limited

Stanley Wong, a.k.a. "anothermountainman", is a renowned designer and artist. His works have been widely exhibited in Hong Kong and abroad. Among them, the "redwhiteblue" series received great acclaim at the 51st Venice Biennale in 2005. Wong won the Best Artist (Visual Arts) Award at the Hong Kong Arts Development Awards 2011, organised by the Hong Kong Arts Development Council.

PP. 180-183

A Beautiful Design

Nominated by Institute of Advertising Singapore as one of the 15 most influential Creative Directors in Singapore for four consecutive years, A Beautiful Design was also awarded Design Agency of the Year at the Creative Circle Awards. Together with six other industry creative leaders, the studio's creative director Roy Poh founded The Design Society, a Singapore-registered, non-profit organisation dedicated to the goals of raising the general standard of design in Singapore.

PP. 110-111

Aaron Nieh Workshop

Aaron Nieh Workshop is among the few most outstanding graphic studios of Taiwan in the past decade, with a body of work seen extensively in the music industry, publications and art-related projects. Its art director Aaron Nieh is most celebrated for his careful arrangement of fonts and his peculiar sensitivity to the various forms of language with their corresponding visuals. Nieh is also a member of AGI.

PP. 244-245

ACST Design

Directed by Albert Cheng-Syun Tang, the design studio specialises in communication design creating works ranging from print to conceptual cross-media projects. ACST's core values are aesthetic, creative, significant and timeless; and the team always endeavours to deliver them in every project.

PP. 118-123

ADDA Studio

Founded by creative director Christian Vögtlin, ADDA is a Stuttgart-based design studio that works in the areas of corporate design, communication and digital media. Apart from the graphic design sector, they also provide strategic consultancy for customers from different industries.

PP. 042-045

Ágnes Herr

Living and working in Budapest, Herr is specialised in graphic design, identity, typography, branding and web design. She is hugely influenced by Carsten Nicolai, Victor Vasarely and Enzo Ragazzini; and her favourite trends are optical art, pop art, science-based arts and other experimental attempts.

PP. 068-069, 178-179

AKU

Based in Tallinn, Estonia, the design agency works across different media with expertise in branding, packaging and spatial design. Founded in 2012 by Alari Orav, Kaarel Kala and Uku-Kristjan Küttis, who share over 35 years of combined experience in graphic design and communications, AKU has enjoyed working with a wide range of clients from long-standing institutions to fresh start-ups, both locally and internationally.

PP. 190-191

Alexia Roux

Based in Montpellier, Roux specialises in visual identity, branding, art direction, print, and web design. The graphic designer is specially passionate for editorial design with great attention to the composition and ratio of the graphic object in its free space. Roux is also sensitive to the materials used for printed objects, their relation to the body and their usage scenarios.

PP. 138-139, 164-167

Anagrama

Specialising in brand development, positioning, and providing creative solutions for any type of project, Anagrama's services reach the entire branding spectrum from strategic consulting to fine tuning brand objectives for the company to logotype, peripherals and captivating illustration design. Besides the history and experience with brand development, the agency also excels in the design and development of objects, spaces and multimedia projects.

PP. 014-015, 060-063, 090-093, 254-257

Anastasia Genkina

A multidisciplinary designer from Moscow, Russia, Genkina graduated in graphic design from the Moscow University of Printing Arts in 2012. She then worked on a renovation project at Gorky Park, freelancing for clients in cultural and business fields ever since.

PP. 230-233

Anonymous

A multidisciplinary studio based in Singapore providing creative direction, content and design. Established in 2005, the studio are the creators of A Design Film Festival, Bracket, plusminusten and the Made in Singapore film. Both partners, Felix Ng and Germaine Chong have been on the jury panel for the British D&AD Awards, Creative Circle Awards and Crowbar Awards.

PP. 034-037

artless Inc.

Establised in 2000 by Shun Kawakami, the interdisciplinary design and consulting firm works across all media including brand design, visual and corporate identity, advertising, packaging, product, video and motion graphics. The studio has won several prestigious international awards including Cannes Gold Lions, NY ADC, D&AD and The London International Award.

PP. 200-201

Asylum

A creative company comprising a design studio, a retail store, a workshop and a record label. Since their inception in 1999, Asylum has worked on cross-disciplinary projects that include interactive design, product development, environmental and interior design, packaging, apparel design, branding and graphic design.

PP. 142-143

Balmer Hählen (formerly A3 Studio)

Founded by Priscilla Balmer and Yvo Hählen, the award-winning Balmer Hählen, which consists of a team of four people, was established since 2013 in the heart of Lausanne. Since its creation, the studio has been involved in collaborations, particularly with designers, stylists and paper shapers. Through design exploration, the studio develops different types of mediums across print, digital and textile materials.

PP. 158-163, 174-175

Blast

Blast focuses on creating and redefining brands using intelligent creativity to help clients stand out and communicate better. Blast believes in the power of great ideas and the difference that good design can be created.

PP. 212-213

BLOW

BLOW is a Hong Kong-based design studio founded by Ken Lo in 2010. Specialising in branding, identities, packaging, environmental graphics, print, publications and website design, they provide clients with mind-blowing yet simple and bold designs that help the brand stand out in the crowd.

PP. 222-229

Bratus

Based in Ho Chi Minh, the branding and strategic creative agency creates bold and memorable work that helps businesses stand proudly apart from their competitors, giving them a long-lasting presence with real integrity.

PP. 066-067

Brian Gartside (DDB New York)

A graduate from Virginia Commonwealth University, Gartside worked at Pentagram before being brought to DDB New York by Menno Kluin and Juan Carlos Pagan in 2012. He became a senior designer at Deutsch Inc, New York in 2014.

PP. 112-113

Bruketa&Zinic OM

One of the leading independent advertising agencies in the world (Campaign, London, 2014) and The Best International Small Agency of the Year (AdAge, Portland, 2013) among others, the agency is one of the most award-winning in Southeastern Europe with over 400 professional awards for advertising and design. It operates in Vienna, Zagreb, Belgrade and Baku, Azerbaijan.

PP. 140-141

Buenos días,

Meaning "Good Morning" in Spanish, the studio consists of Javier R. Calvo and Jorge Augusto. With a focus in the cultural sector, the duo is interested in small projects, taking care of editing, working on every detail and dialogues with clients. Calvo and Augusto are paper lovers who always want to emphasise the value of it through their work, especially in this digital age.

PP. 114-115

Bureau Hardy Seiler

Hardy Seiler is a designer, an art director and the founder of the award-winning Bureau Hardy Seiler – a design studio for corporate, editorial, graphic- and web design. The studio often joins forces with other experts to solve more complex challenges.

PP. 088-089

Bureau Rabensteiner

Rabensteiner is an Austrian design studio specialising in creative direction and graphic design. Since day one, Rabensteiner has always been about quality and detail.

PP. 026-029

Büro North

Established in 2004, Büro North is an interdisciplinary design practice delivering evidence-based solutions that are creative, measurable and meaningful. Led by design director Soren Luckins and wayfinding director Finn Butler, the diverse team works across the disciplines of graphic design, industrial design and wayfinding.

PP. 168-169

Carlos Bermúdez, Mau Morgó

After graduating from Eina School of Arts and Design Barcelona in 2009, Bermúdez and Morgó both joined the award-winning agency Mucho and started their online inspiration platform "We Die for Beauty". They now run their own studio, focusing in print, motion, and art installations.

PP. 170-173

Chad Michael Studio

An independent branding and packaging design studio that specialises in liquor design and unique branding.

PP. 264-265

COMMUNE

A creative team based in Sapporo, Japan specialising in graphic design. Motivated by the will to make things better, COMMUNE works to encourage people and the society for a change. At times, their creations take people by surprise, awaken their emotions, or even move them to tears.

PP. 188-189

Csönge Balla

A freelance graphic designer based in Budapest. After finishing her MA in sociology at the Eötvös Loránd Science University, Balla went on to study graphic design at the Hungarian University of Fine Arts. She likes to promote social issues through her design, and hopes to combine it with her sociology background in her future work.

PP. 262-263, 270-271

Demian Conrad Design

Created in 2007, the Demian Conrad Design studio is based in Lausanne. Working mainly in the cultural field, the studio lends its expertise to everything related to events communication and visual identity. It is currently exploring alternative methods that use traditional printing and new cutting-edge digital printing techniques.

PP. 030-033

DENTSU INC.

DENTSU INC. has a diverse client portfolio and enjoys solid buying power in all major mass media formats. The company handles the advertising campaigns of many blue-chip companies, and major global clients have chosen the company as their partner in the Japanese market. Hideto Yagi joined DENTSU in 2006 as art director and graphic designer, and expanded his playing field while working for clients including Uniqlo, Honda, Fuji Film, Kirin and Nestlé.

PP. 070-073

DENTSU INC. CHUBU

DENTSU is the No.1 advertising company in the Japanese market. DENTSU INC. CHUBU is the most powerful branch of DENTSU inc., winning at Cannes, CLIO, NY Festival, Spikes and the like.

PP. 102-105

Edited

Established in 2011 by Wu Cheuk-pan, the Hong Kong-based studio specialises in publication and identity design.

PP. 106-107

Enserio

Aiming to transmit the most with the least, Enserio is a group of graphic designers from Banyoles who are serious but creative, transgressive perfectionists. They are fans of manual processes and limited editions. Their style is to work in groups and organise workshops. They also love to move by bike and play ping-pong.

PP. 278-279

Eszter Laki

A graduate of the Hungarian University of Fine Arts where she studied graphics, Laki later participated in a typography course at Moholy-Nagy University of Art and Design. Laki's primary field of design is branding and packaging design. An image designer for numerous clubs and restaurants like Tokio, Terminál Restaurant and Kolor, she is also the creator of many limited edition fine-food product-packaging and branding.

PP. 266-267

Éva Valicsek

Valicsek graduated in packaging design from the Institute Of Applied Art at Moholy-Nagy University of Art and Design Budapest Sopron, Hungary.

PP. 108-109

Firebelly Design

Committed to cultivating connections between human beings and ideas, inspiring conscious thoughts and actions, Firebelly works as early advocates of socially responsible design pioneering an ethic that values honesty, empathy and Good Design for a Good Reason. A group of skilled typographers, writers, photographers and makers with over 75 combined years of experience, Firebelly provides each client with insightful design tailored specifically to their needs.

PP. 124-127

Foreign Policy Design Group

Helmed by creative directors Yah-Leng Yu and Arthur Chin, the group works on projects ranging from creative/art direction and design, branding, brand strategy, digital strategy, strategic research and marketing campaign services for luxury fashion and lifestyle brands, fast-moving consumer goods, arts and cultural institutions as well as think tank consultancies.

PP. 076-079

Four Plus Studio

Working to provide meaningful design solutions, the studio believes individual approach is the key to the specific needs of every project. They deeply value close and honest collaboration with their partners.

PP. 268-269

Graphic design studio by Yurko Gutsulyak

Born in 1979 in Ukraine with an academic background in economics, Gutsulyak began his design career when he moved to Kiev in 2001. He founded his studio in 2005. As the winner of more than 30 international awards, he was elected as the first president of Art Directors Club Ukraine in 2010.

PP. 246-247

Happycentro

Founded in 1998 in Verona, Happycentro has worked for both big and small clients. Mixing complexity and order is their formula for beauty. The team always spends plenty of energy in research and testing on visual art, typography, graphic design, illustration, animation, film direction and music besides commissioned work.

PP. 134-135, 154-155

Hey

A multidisciplinary design studio based in Barcelona specialising in brand management, editorial design, packaging- and interactive design, Hey shares the profound conviction that good design means combining content, functionality, graphical expression and strategy.

PP. 040-041, 050-051

IYA Studio

IYA Studio works across various design disciplines from its base in London. The team brings a wealth of experience to each project with an in-depth understanding of many fields, allowing it to deliver work that is cohesive and consistent, from online retail touchpoints to print and interiors.

PP. 216-217

Jin Ping Soh

Soh is a graphic designer based in Singapore who finds the design process tantamount to storytelling. His practice aims at communicating stories through the re-presentation of forms and languages. Soh enjoys a multitude of designs ranging from environmental to experiential, publication, and branding. He has received awards and mentions from the likes of Crowbar Awards, Singapore and For Print Only.

PP. 116-117

Kanella

A former graphic design student in Athens who later mastered in communication design at Central Saint Martins, Kanella Arapoglou mainly works for and collaborates with prestigious design agencies undertaking projects for the publishing and music industries. Currently, Arapoglou is devoted to her own creative studio in Greece and teaching at the Technological Educational Institute in Athens.

PP. 210-211

Kuan-li Tang, Cavis Huang, Jhih-ting Chen

Graduates from the Oriental Institute of Technology, Taiwan. While Tang and Huang studied Industrial and Commercial Design, Chen took the Industry Management course. Tang is more focused on conceptual design, production and photography; Huang specialises in illustration; whereas Chen works mostly on directing films and post-production.

PP. 148-151

LENS ASSOCIATES INC.

The Nagoya-based studio was founded by graphic designer Masao Shirasawa who was awarded a New York ADC Bronze and many other prizes for his illustrations. In 2014, he won the grand prize at the first Cannes Lions Health for his design for Mother Book, as well as a Gold Cannes Lions, a One Show Gold Pencil, and a Gold Clio Award.

PP. 098-101

Leo Burnett, Dept. of Design

Founded in 2009 as a small department within the Leo Burnett agency offering expertise in the intersection of concept, craft and storytelling, their work focuses on four agency efforts: campaign development, corporate branding, philanthropic work and brand extension.

PP. 192-193

Lundgren+Lindqvist

Lundgren+Lindqvist is a Swedish design studio led by founding partners Andreas Friberg Lundgren and Carl-Johan Lindqvist. Using a conceptually-driven approach, it has built an international reputation for crafting high-quality solutions that are equally compelling to the eyes and the intellect. The duo also runs Il'Editions, a publishing platform and imprint for creative cross-disciplinary collaborations.

PP. 086-087

LWZ

LWZ is a design and animation studio based in Vienna that experiments with unconventional approaches, causing visual derailments with happy endings.

PP. 186-187

MAAN Design Studio

Founded in 2011, MANN is an independent multidisciplinary studio with Portuguese heritage, based in Vila do Conde. Formed by Pedro Lima Ferreira and Vitor Claro who are both enthusiastic in communication design, MANN works with a personal project methodology that is attentive to the uniqueness of technical, aesthetic and ethical details.

PP. 046-049

Manual

A design and visual communication studio in San Francisco, Manual works with a broad range of clients from startups to the world's most revered brands across print, packaging and digital media. Manual's work strives to uncover the intangible essence of a brand and express it through unique visual solutions, helping businesses and organisations articulate their unique offerings.

PP. 052-055

MARKS

A contemporary graphic design agency that focuses on corporate communications in the luxury, art and industry sectors, as well as with public institutions. MARKS goes straight to the point and works with imaginative and demanding approaches.

PP. 056-059

Marton Borzak

Marton Borzak is a graphic designer who studied at the Royal Danish Academy of Fine Arts, School of Design and the Hungarian University of Fine Arts. He gained his professional experience in Budapest, Copenhagen and New York working with various clients including banks and startups.

PP. 094-097

Max Molitor, Cajza Nydén

Molitor and Nydén are studying packaging design at Broby Grafiska in Sweden.

PP. 258-259

mistroom

Co-founded by Peng Yu-jui and Huang Jui-i in 2010, mistroom is a design studio that stays sensitive to a certain design aesthetic that reveals the true essence of daily life, and elegantly evokes its viewers' senses and memories.

PP. 084-085

Mubien

Mubien is a full-service branding studio focused on helping companies become fully themselves. The team blends simplicity with sophistication to create elegant, powerful and timeless identities.

PP. 016-021

Naonori Yago

Born in Shizuoka, Naonori Yago is an art director and graphic designer who has won awards from the Tokyo and New York ADCs, D&AD, Cannes Lions, and the One Show. He graduated from the Department of Visual Communication Design, Musashino Art University in 2009.

PP. 194-195

nendo

Founded by architect Oki Sato in 2002 in Tokyo, nendo holds its goal of bringing small surprises to people through multidisciplinary practices of different media including architecture, interiors, furniture, industrial products and graphic design.

PP. 236-241

NOSIGNER

NOSIGNER is a social design activist that drives change towards a more hopeful future. Using design as a tool to form meaningful relationships, the studio creates multidisciplinary strategies by seeking the highest quality within each design field, including architecture, product and graphic design.

PP. 176-177

Oddds

Founded in 2013 by designers based in Penang and Singapore respectively, Oddds focuses on graphic design, branding, photography, publication design and illustration. Their work reflects significantly on behaviours, including how it draws attention and how it influences people, while the team believes in aesthetics and futurism.

PP. 064-065

ONOGRIT

Founded by award-winning designers, Janina Braun and Daniela Kempkes, the creative consultancy and design studio is based on the principle that design is not only an aesthetic style, but ambitious problem-solving. The duo successfuly ran ARE WE DESIGNER for 10 years before the startup of ONOGRIT.

PP. 184-185

OUWN

OUWN was founded as a corporation in 2013 by Atsushi Ishiguro and Munechika Fujita. The name stems from the hope to foster interaction and dialogue by sharing the business that the duo owns ("OWN") with you ("U"). This objective has previously formed the basis of their design project — a cultural exhibition where creators from their generation gather with a shared interest in design and music as the focal point.

PP. 130-131

Paperlux GmbH

Based in Hamburg, Paperlux GmbH is a design studio with a staff of nine specialising in branding, corporate design, editorial design, event communication, typography, illustration, art, spatial communication, etc.

PP. 250-253, 276-277

Philip Stroomberg

Born in 1967, the Amsterdam-based graphic designer works primarily in the cultural sector. His clients include universities, publishers, and art institutions. Stroomberg regularly creates designs that are used to promote Dutch culture. An important feature of his work is interaction which encourages users to develop a bond with the related object and often challenges the user's imagination.

PP. 274-275

Power-nap Over

Founded in Hong Kong by Vita Mak in 2013, the studio works across a diverse range of projects including art direction, branding, editorial, event, packaging and website design. The team also develops their home products and independent publications. They intend to use products, graphics and text to express opinions about living.

PP. 132-133

Raw Color

Christoph Brach and Daniera ter Haar started Raw Color in 2008 after graduating from the Design Academy Eindhoven. Their work reflects a sophisticated treatment of material by mixing the fields of photography and graphic design, with the materialisation of colour as the core. They mainly work in cultural and design-related fields.

PP. 038-039

Rice Creative

The Ho Chi Minh City-based creative agency was founded in 2011 by Joshua Breiden Bach and Chi-An De Lep, creating honest and powerful creative solutions. The pair's background in branding, packaging, digital and developing 360 advertising campaigns offers the opportunity to craft world-class concepts for a select spectrum of clients.

PP. 234-235

Acknowledgements

We would like to thank all the designers and companies who have involved in the production of this book. This project would not have been accomplished without their significant contribution to the compilation of this book. We would also like to express our gratitude to all the producers for their invaluable opinions and assistance throughout this entire project. The successful completion also owes a great deal to many professionals in the creative industry who have given us precious insights and comments. And to the many others whose names are not credited but have made specific input in this book, we thank you for your continuous support the whole time.

Future Editions

If you wish to participate in viction:ary's future projects and publications, please send your website or portfolio to submit@victionary.com

Somewhere Else

Somewhere Else provides distilled solutions that translate strategy into visuals inextricably adding value to businesses. Together with a broad range of clients, the studio continually pushes to create unique works that are idea-driven, relevant, long-lasting and intelligently crafted, be it through branding, art direction, wayfinding systems or anything in between.

PP. 136-137, 248-249

Studio Hausherr

A small graphic design agency based in Berlin that focuses on corporate, editorial and web design for clients in the fields of art, fashion and culture. The studio provides a comprehensive design and visual communication tailored to suit their needs.

PP. 208-209

Studio Much

Believing that concept and practice are a duality between fantasy and reality, the studio aims to bridge the gap, generating sound ideas and transforming them into inspiring, well-crafted designs. Founded and directed in 2010 by Times Pang following his graduation in fine art from Academy of Art University, San Francisco, their work is recognised by Type Director's Club, New York and HKDA, Hong Kong.

PP. 128-129, 260-261

studioKALEIDO

A progressive, full-service design practice and curatorial think-tank. Founder Winnie Wu is amongst the few most outstanding designers of Singapore with a body of work largely focused in the arts industry. Profiled as a top creative talent in Asia, she is best known for her peculiar sensitivity and innovation in print design and typography.

PP. 152-153

StudioMakgill

An independent design studio working with businesses and cultural organisations large and small, StudioMakgill focuses on the creation of brand identities and visual communication providing succinct, innovative, beautiful solutions that last, inspire and enable clients to realise their ambitions.

PP. 202-203

studiowmw

studiowmw is a Hong Kong-based multidisciplinary design studio that was founded in 2013. Its services revolve around branding, print, products, packaging, exhibitions, installations and websites for the community, culture and commerce. The 'w.m.w.' in its name stands for 'we do what is most wanted, and collaborate to achieve better'.

PP. 218-221

The Bakery Design Studio

A Moscow-based independent creative practice with a global reach, the studio specialises in branding, visual identity and graphic design. In just three years, Bakery has successfully established itself as a prominent figure on the international design scene working with both huge international companies and small local start-ups from over the world.

PP. 272-273

The Folks Studio

Working across all possible platforms, providing design and consultancy services in the fields of graphic, communication, branding, product, spatial and digital design, The Folks Studio is a design practice based in Singapore founded by Soon Siewhui and Yang Zhengliang in 2012.

PP. 080-081

UMA/design farm

Founded by art director and designer Yuma Harada in 2007, UMA/design farm works to provide book design, graphic design, exhibition design, space design, and also total art direction.

PP. 204-205

viction workshop ltd.

Established to emphasise the strength of collaborative efforts in the area of visual communication, viction:ary creates multiple dimensions for the understanding of design and visual graphics as a channel for creative talents to share their truest spirits with people from around the world.

PP. 144-147

Xavi Martínez

The Barcelona-based graphic designer graduated from ESDi with his final degree project Vaques Sagrades winning a Gold Laus Award in 2014. Martínez was an intern at ruiz+company, the head of the graphic design department of the ESDi University, and a junior graphic designer at Artofmany. He is now with Bunch and also works independently on a broad range of projects.

PP. 206-207

Zeynep Orbay

A Turkish graphic designer currently living and working in Amsterdam, Orbay has received many national and international design awards including One Show, D&AD, Cannes Lions, Eurobest and a Grand Prix in the design category.

PP. 242-243

Zuzanna Rogatty

A freelancer studying graphic design in the University of Art in Poznan, Rogatty always tries to be original in every project, paying attention to all details. Rogatty believes design is a specific solution to a task or a problem, and should not be bounded by fashion or trends that lead to the same end. Rogatty thinks the content is what matters, not only the visuals.

PP. 074-075